STRESSMAP
FINDING YOUR PRESSURE POINTS

C. Michele Haney

and

Edmond W. Boenisch, Jr.

Impact Publishers
POST OFFICE BOX 1094
SAN LUIS OBISPO, CALIFORNIA 93406

First Edition, August, 1982
Second Edition, February, 1987   Third Printing, May, 1991

Copyright © 1982, 1987
by C. Michele Haney and Edmond W. Boenisch, Jr.

All rights reserved under International and Pan-American Copyright Conventions. No part of this book may be reproduced, stored in a retrieval system, or transmitted in any form or by any means, electronic, mechanical, photocopying, recording or otherwise, without express written permission of the authors or publisher, except for (1) brief quotations in critical reviews, and (2) single copies for personal use of the "StressMap" questionnaires the composite "StressMap", the "Planning Worksheet," and the "Stress Management Plan."

"The Born Loser," "Frank and Ernest" and "Eek and Meek" are reproduced in the text by permission of Newspaper Enterprise Association, © 1981 and 1982.

Library of Congress Cataloging in Publication Data

Haney, C. Michele, 1944-
  Stress map.

  Bibliography: p.
  1. Stress (Psychology)   I. Boenisch, Edmond W.,
1947-   . II. Title.
BF575.S75H37   1982   158'.1   82-15391
ISBN 0-915166-60-7 (pbk.)

PUBLISHER'S NOTE

This publication is designed to provide accurate and authoritative information in regard to the subject matter covered. It is sold with the understanding that the publisher is not engaged in rendering psychological, medical, or other professional services. If expert assistance or counseling is needed, the services of a competent professional should be sought.

Cover design and illustrations by Rob Sexton

Back cover photos: L. Stephenson
Printed in the United States of America

Published by **Impact Publishers**
POST OFFICE BOX 1094
SAN LUIS OBISPO, CALIFORNIA 93406

CONTENTS

1. What Is This Thing Called Stress? 1
2. ...And How Was *Your* Day? 9
3. People StressMap 17
4. Money StressMap 22
5. Work StressMap 25
6. Leisure StressMap 31
7. Mind StressMap 34
8. Body StressMap 40
9. Your Life StressMap 47
10. Life Stress Planning 57
11. People Stress Buffers 63
12. Money Stress Buffers 70
13. Work Stress Buffers 74
14. Leisure Stress Buffers 81
15. Mind Stress Buffers 90
16. Body Stress Buffers 95
17. Stress Relief: Relaxation 100
18. Stress Relief: Eating Habits 109
19. Stress Relief: Physical Fitness 123
20. Stress Relief: Assertiveness and
    Time Management 127
21. Stress Relief: Avoiding Burnout 138
Suggested Readings 150

You can make a choice about your stress...

...to live...

"...the healer inside us is the wisest, most complex, integrated entity in the universe."
          Marilyn Ferguson
          The Aquarian Conspiracy

...or to die...

"...the human body...is capable of literally destroying itself when it is forced to maintain a high stress alarm state for long periods without relief."
          Karl Albrecht
          Stress and the Manager

...We hope you choose wisely every day.

Introduction

A decade ago, stress was just another word in the dictionary. The corporate ulcer was an isolated status symbol—the price of success. High blood pressure, heart attacks, and strokes were the misfortunes of only a few.

The world has changed too much, too fast. Or is it that your ability to cope with that world has changed too slowly, too late? Can you really continue to match your body against the speed of the new world that greets you every morning?

New devices appeared in the fifties, sixties and seventies, so accurate, and so accessible that they promised to allow you to do all your work in less time. You would have a wealth of leisure hours to spare. The concern back then was how you would deal with all that extra time. Remember that?

Technology did keep its promise. The machines did help you to do much more in much less time. But somehow, instead of using the available hours for leisure and relaxation, the American public realized that even more could be crammed into each day. The race was on; the goals: competitive advantage, profits, and "success."

The most obvious outcome of the race, however, was *stress*. What's more, it is no longer the by-product of work alone. We have allowed stress to creep into every part of our lifestyle. We seem to thrive on pressure wherever it can be found. Some even take great pride in their stress; it is the new badge of courage from a strange society.

You are probably reading this because you recognize the need to do something to achieve a more liveable, more human existence. Your challenge is called *stress management.* Not yet a national priority, it is a personal decision for each of us.

Stress can be controlled. You need only understand the process that *causes* stress, be aware of *how distressed* you are, recognize the *sources* of your stress, become *motivated* enough to change, *learn how* to change, and *follow through.* The purpose of this book is to help you with each step.

Specifically, you will have the opportunity to:
- Learn about the signs, effects, and causes of stress,
- Identify the sources of your stress,
- Identify resources and stress management techniques that can be used to decrease distress, and
- Formulate a tentative plan and action steps to prevent or alleviate some of the distress in your own life.

Stress can be a positive factor in your life. Wouldn't you rather have it that way?

1
What Is This Thing Called Stress?

If you are alive, you will experience stress. No one is immune. Like it or not, stress is going to be with you every day. You are constantly reacting to people and events in your life.

Touching a hot element on a stove or hearing a good joke both cause reactions. Each actually produces a type of stress. Stress occurs whenever the mind and body react to some real or imagined threatening event or situation. Events which cause stress reactions are called *stressors*.

Some stress is beneficial or desirable. Other types of stress, particularly if prolonged, can fatigue or damage your system to the point of malfunction or disease. Since all conditions or events in everyday life cause some type or degree of stress, the object is not to totally eliminate stress from your life! You actually *need* moderate levels of stress to help you stay alert and perform well. The only people totally free of stress are those who populate our cemeteries!

Dr. Hans Selye, the "father" of stress research, made the important distinction between stress which is harmful and that which is beneficial. Harmful stress can cause one to feel helpless, frustrated, disappointed. It can also cause either physical or psychological damage. Selye called this *distress*. Other types of stress are beneficial and give a sense of achievement or exhilaration. Such stress, which is pleasant and helps us to live effectively, he termed *eustress*.

It is not so much the stressor itself or the intensity of the stressor that makes stress beneficial or detrimental, but the *personal reaction* to the event or condition. A good example is flying: Some people enjoy it tremendously and experience eustress, while others become frightened or even hysterical and feel distress.

We are not born with undesirable reactions to stressors. We learn—by watching others, by parental demands, by painful coincidences, etc.—how to react to different situations, and eventually develop habits that persist. In Chapter 2, you will meet two persons who experience the same stressors. One is successful in stress management and competently transforms stress into a positive force. The other tends to be out of control, reacting to stressors and allowing life to be distressed. What kind of reactions to stress have you learned?

The Universal Instinctive, Primitive Stress Reaction

When you encounter a stressor, your whole body responds. A biological reaction occurs that includes your muscles, gastrointestinal system, brain, cardiovascular system, and skin. This reaction upsets the normal balance of your body but is meant to help you deal with the stressors in an effective and fast way.

Consider what you would feel and think if one night your sound sleep were disturbed by a strange sound you *think* you heard. You live alone. You are not sure if you heard anything. Sometimes the house does make strange noises on a cold, windy winter's night. Maybe you were dreaming. You lie very still and listen for a few agonizing minutes to make sure it was not a dream. You hear the sound again. You are sure now that there are footsteps in the next room! The stress response begins with your *thought process* which triggers a chain reaction in your body. In this situation you would *not* experience any stress if you did not wake up.

Since you are awake, the process, extremely simplified, may go like this:

An electrical message in the brain stimulates your pituitary gland, a very small gland located in the brain. The pituitary gland excretes a hormone, ACTH (*a*dreno*c*ortico*t*ropic *h*ormone) into the bloodstream. ACTH flows to two glands located just above your kidneys, the adrenals, which increase their secretion of adrenalin and a series of other hormones, causing your body to become highly aroused, ready for action. The chemical change affects every cell in your body. This whole electrical and chemical process takes only about eight seconds!

At the same time other electrical messages in the nerves cause changes in your heart, lungs, and muscles. Your whole body is quickly placed on alert, ready to react. Your tiny blood vessels constrict, raising your blood pressure and supplying your muscles with a rich supply of blood. Muscle tone increases dramatically, ready for quick and effective action. Remember the stories about men and women in highly stressful emergencies performing unbelievable physical feats, such as lifting automobiles? Your liver begins to quickly produce glucose which is a needed energy source for your brain and muscles. Your breathing rate quickens, which increases the oxygen supply in the blood so your muscles and brain can use the glucose more effectively. Your heart rate speeds up, increasing the amount of blood sent to different parts of your body. The parts that need more blood, your brain and muscles, are given top priority, while blood is diverted from other less critical organs such as your stomach and intestines. This basically interrupts digestion, which is why under prolonged stress you may have digestive problems. Your brain especially needs a more abundant supply of glucose-rich blood so it can increase its electrical activity and better control your body's actions. Blood is also diverted from your hands and feet. Not only does this allow more blood to be used where it is needed (brain, large muscles, heart) but this action would also minimize excessive bleeding if your extremities were injured. A negative side effect: your hands and feet may become cold and clammy under stress.

In this highly stressful situation, your hearing becomes more acute. The pupils of your eyes dilate, increasing your vision sensitivity. The concentration of the clotting agent in your blood even increases. These last few body changes occur to help you prepare for a physical struggle. They are evolutionary remnants from your biological past, but in certain life or death situations these stress reactions are invaluable.

This whole process is a magnificently coordinated electrical and chemical alerting of your body for a possible fight-or-flight response. How intense this reaction is, or how long it lasts, all depends on how stressful or serious you perceive the situation to be. The process occurs quickly (in about eight to ten seconds), unconsciously, and yet is a very normal response of your body to protect itself against possible harm.

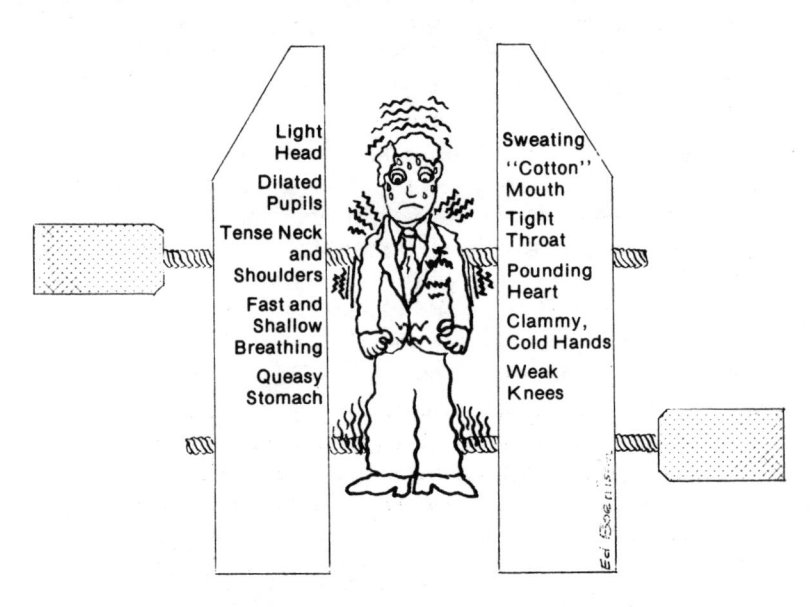

Light Head
Dilated Pupils
Tense Neck and Shoulders
Fast and Shallow Breathing
Queasy Stomach

Sweating
"Cotton" Mouth
Tight Throat
Pounding Heart
Clammy, Cold Hands
Weak Knees

There is a great deal more to be said about stress, of course. We have kept this discussion brief so you may move quickly into the process of finding and relieving your own debilitating stress. If you wish to pursue the emotional and physical systems of stress in greater depth, we encourage you to read Dr. Selye's work—and that of other key researchers in the field—described in the "Suggested Readings" at the end of this book.

Can Stress Really Kill?

Your stress response is automatically called into action every time you experience or think about something threatening. There is no in-between; it is an all-or-nothing reaction. A stress response occurs in an automobile accident and will probably recur each time one relives the experience in memory. The body does not make a distinction between real and imagined events. In a life-and-death situation, this unconscious, quick reaction associated with the stress response can be critical to survival. In every stress reaction, your brain and your body are mobilized and ready for immediate action. You have the choice of fight or flight or no action. But just stewing in your stressful "juices" (not acting) can also be harmful.

Your stress response fails you when it does not adapt to the severity of a real situation. This imperfect way of coping with every real or imagined threat eventually takes its toll in the form of stress-induced diseases, or diseases of adaptation. If you are not managing your stress responses to avoid distress and achieve eustress, you may be laying the groundwork for diseases of maladaptation—and even death.

> "...some diseases in which stress usually plays a particularly important role are high blood pressure, cardiac accidents, gastric or duodenal ulcers (the 'stress ulcers'), and various types of mental disturbances."
>
> Hans Selye
> *Stress Without Distress*

"Although occasionally some of the claims are extreme and at times even unsupported by sound research, this should in no way confuse the basic fact: Stress can cause or seriously aggravate a variety of body problems and illnesses. This statement is substantiated by extensive research in the fields of physiology and medicine and by years of experience by well-respected practitioners in all fields of physical health and physiology."

Herbert Greenberg
Coping with Job Stress

"Very few, if any diseases are 'caused' in isolation by one factor....Rather than conclude that any disorder is 'caused' solely by stress, we should think of stress as being one of the important variables in the body's operation....Ulcers are a well-known example of stress-related disorders....Heart attack...is an infamous stress-linked disorder....Digestive disorders such as colitis, spastic colon, gastritis, and chronic diarrhea and constipation are very sensitive to stress levels....Although this listing of stress linked diseases could go on and on, this brief summary makes a very strong point: that the human body—your body—is capable of literally destroying itself when it is forced to maintain a high stress alarm state for long periods without relief."

Karl Albrecht
Stress and the Manager

"Stress-induced disorders have long since replaced epidemics of infectious disease as the major medical problem of the post-industrial nations. During recent years, four disorders have become especially prominent in the United States, Western Europe, and Japan. Described as the afflictions of civilization, they are cardiovascular disorders, cancer, arthritis, and respiratory diseases (including bronchitis and emphysema)."

Kenneth Pelletier
Mind as Healer, Mind as Slayer

WHAT IS STRESS?

Some physiological disorders that are often stress-related are:

- pounding of the heart
- ulcers
- heart attacks
- strokes
- cancer
- hypertension (high blood pressure)
- headaches/migraine headaches
- digestive disorders (colitis, spastic colon, gastritis, chronic diarrhea or constipation, frequent urination, queasiness and sometimes vomiting)
- arthritis
- tooth decay
- backache
- chronic fatigue
- insomnia or poor sleeping habits
- rashes
- loss or excessive appetite
- diabetes
- infections
- allergies
- fainting spells
- feeling of dizziness
- trembling/nervous tics
- stuttering and other speech difficulties
- grinding of the teeth
- premenstrual tension or missed periods
- sweating
- muscle aches/tension

Believe it or not, even BASIC AGING is in part a result of the stress of everyday living taking its toll on the whole body.

Psychologically, stress may affect you. You may experience:

- apathy
- regression
- withdrawal
- forgetfulness
- anxiety
- depression
- emotional tension and alertness (being "keyed up")
- nightmares
- high-pitched nervous laughter
- dissatisfactions
- irritability
- poor concentration
- accident-proneness
- an overpowering urge to cry or run and hide
- tendency to be easily startled by small sounds

Stress and its harmful effects also affect the immune system. In a normal state this system seeks out and destroys harmful viruses and bacteria. When stress is experienced, the hormones released can alter the healthy functioning of your immune system, resulting in a susceptibility to the viruses and bacteria around you. This could explain why you *may* contract the common cold, flu, and infections that you would normally resist in unstressed living.

If you complain about too much stress in your life, you are feeling *your own undesirable reactions* and the *effects* of stress. Can you change your behavior? Perhaps not, if you have lived with detrimental stress (distress) too long even to recognize the results. Or you may see the results and feel overwhelmed and powerless.

Many people who have too much stress change their behavior, usually rapidly, after the heart attack. Others recognize the effects of stress, systematically analyze the stressors in their lives and take positive action *before* the heart attack occurs.

2
...And How Was *Your* Day?

Despite its physical symptoms, and the universal human reactions we all share, there are some *individual* responses to stress. The "typical day" described below for two very different people is an example:

On Tuesday, the 30th of February, cousins D.I. Stress and E.U. Stress both awoke with a start. Their respective alarm clocks had failed, and each was an hour late. Here is how the day went:

E.U. Stress and D.I. Stress in Action

STRESSORS	DISTRESS	EUSTRESS
Alarm did not go off. One hour late.	Angry, upset, worried. Rush to get ready. Make mistakes and lose more time.	Start to get upset but realize extra sleep felt good and it's not a daily occurrence. Use deep breathing exercise while dressing quickly.
Carpool ride arrives.	Snap at friend, both lose temper. Breathing rate increases. Feel out of control.	Ask friend to call other rider and explain unfortunate delay. Grab oranges to share with friends in car.

STRESSMAP

Encounter heavy traffic. More time lost.	Become irritated at traffic. Cause everyone to get upset. Complain about lousy day.	Discuss with others how you will adjust appointments. Talk slowly and confidently. Take time to compose self for rest of day.
Meet first appointment 20 minutes late.	Try to rush through work. Make mistakes. Gripe about how badly the day started. Drop pen and bump head picking it up. Face becomes contorted and stays tense. Client becomes uneasy.	Apologize for inconvenience. Concentrate on relaxing muscles while listening closely to client. Have productive interview even though still behind schedule.
Lunch hour delayed.	Eat quickly. Do not talk to anyone. Do not enjoy meal. Rush back to office with beginning of indigestion.	Call colleague before eating to inform him about 15 minute delay. Eat slowly, thinking about favorite hiking spot. Stop and wash face before going to meeting.
Driving home in carpool.	Remember hassles of day. Tell fellow riders about all the problems. Stomach still upset. Shoulder and neck stiff. Headache starting. All feel uneasy.	Since not driving, take time to close eyes for few minutes and relax muscles. Plan a peaceful evening as a way of being good to yourself for challenging day.
Evening at home.	Gulp down a stiff drink. Feel angry about day. Rush through supper. Stomp around house. Kick dog.	Take a long, soaking bath. Fix favorite meal while listening to favorite album. Eat slowly. Spend time with pet.
Bedtime.	Get angry again when setting alarm. Take 45 minutes to fall asleep. Muscles still tight. Toss and turn all night.	Read a favorite novel in bed after making mental note of positive happenings of day. Drift off to sleep relaxed and calm.

Quite a day, wasn't it? D.I. Stress was really running, right from the beginning. Yet, although just as late, old "E.U." seemed to take it all in stride, making something positive out of each event as the day progressed. The difference was in their own *responses* to the stress condition. D.I. literally "fought" through every step, while E.U. accepted the situation for what it was: an inconvenience to be dealt with as comfortably as possible...for herself and those around her.

Some stress researchers have described a similar, although not exactly parallel, model to the Selye distress-eustress system. Meyer Friedman and Ray H. Rosenman are San Francisco physicians who have studied heart attack victims for many years. They describe two general types of lifestyles which seem to separate victims from non-victims. "Type A" persons are those who react to stressors as D.I. did: time-urgent, achievement-oriented, aggressive and fast. "Type B" persons are more like "E.U." in that they exhibit less "hurry sickness" and enjoy a more relaxed outlook on life.

Type A individuals, of course, do gain many of society's rewards. Success in business, for example, if measured by sales volume, rapid promotion, or public recognition is often a result of Type A behavior. The key question, of course, is "Is it really *worth* it?" Let us dispel a common myth about Type B: *They are just as successful, competent and goal-oriented as Type A!* They just go about it with less hurry and fuss.

Friedman and Rosenman provide an extensive profile in their book. Here are just a few Type A characteristics:
- Always moves, walks, eats rapidly.
- Tells and shows impatience because events take place too slowly. Tries to hurry the speech of others.
- Tries to perform or think about two or more things at once.
- Feels guilty relaxing.
- Does not have any spare time to develop as a person; too busy acquiring and accumulating things.

- Schedules more and more in less and less time without allowing for the unpredictable.*

Becoming Type B and Living Longer

You will find that you can change many Type A habits to Type B without endangering your "success." And you'll greatly improve your chance to stay alive! If you have found that you are deeply ingrained in the Type A pattern, try to begin to change by "impersonating" the Type B person. Here are some suggestions (you'll find many more in later chapters of this book!):
- Find pleasure in the simple activities of life without feeling it necessary to "justify" playfulness.
- Develop and maintain a high level of physical fitness.
- Balance overloads and crises at work with breathing periods.
- Provide yourself with escape routes for occasional detachment and relaxation.
- Make a concerted effort to walk, speak, and eat slowly.
- Look for ways to add laughter to your life.
- Admit that it is not your responsibility to make everything go right in the lives of those around you.
- Enjoy those yellow lights while driving. Try some relaxation exercises while you are waiting.

Type B's have the ability to bring a creative balance to work and play. So can you!

Planning a program for behavior change requires a high level of awareness of behavior patterns. In analyzing your behavior patterns, you not only learn more about your thoughts or feelings that may stimulate your behavior but also how to recognize the social and physical environment cues that similarly influence your action.

---

*Adapted from Friedman and Rosenman, *Type A Behavior and Your Heart*, pp. 100-102.

Behavior patterns are complex and sometimes the future may look bleak when considering the prospects of changing them. We admit, it's not easy. But the payoff—a longer, healthier, happier life—is worth much more than the "cost." What's more, people who have made similar changes in their lives report that it's not really as tough as it looks, once you commit yourself and actually get started.

The purpose of *StressMap* is to give you some "handles" on your own lifestyle, and to point out the proven ways you can begin to bring about the changes you would like. We've adopted a "holistic" approach. Something of a buzz word these days, "holistic" simply means we've tried to look at you as a *complete* person, not just a body, or a mind, or a job, or any other of your parts. The next section will help explain what we mean.

What is This "Holistic" Approach to Stress Management?

Holistic health is somewhat difficult to describe; it is not a specific medication, treatment, or therapy of the varieties usually associated with staying healthy. Holistic health is a personal attitude and lifestyle oriented toward health and healing. It emphasizes such concepts as *wellness* and *preventive care*. Most importantly, the holistic approach concentrates on your responsibility for your own personal well-being and happiness.

Holistic health is not merely concerned with the physical as the key to staying well. It recognizes that you are a balance of the physical, mental, spiritual and social. To some degree stress can be found in each of these areas of life. But stress, no matter where it is, disrupts healthy functioning. Your whole life cycle is affected. So it is not surprising that stress reduction and stress management are critical keys to achieving and maintaining complete health.

Listening to your body and mind is important both to general health and to stress management. If you ignore stresses in your life, your mind and body may take action "on their own" and cause physical or psychological illness. The human mind and body will try to heal themselves, literally pulling you out of the action and getting you away from the stress—by creating illness if that's what it takes!

The holistic approach to stress management requires that you take responsibility for your own health, physically, mentally, spiritually and socially. You must recognize the stressors in each area of your life, then admit you have alternatives. You are not a powerless victim of others or the outside world. The stressors are always going to be there, but your own thought processes and reactions will determine how you are affected. What you *think* determines how you *feel* and *act*.

Managing your stress means taking control and learning how to use your mind to determine what happens to your body. You know that people can think themselves *sick,* yet how many people do you know who have ever tried to think themselves *well*? Have *you* ever done it?

We urge you to become responsible for your own personal well-being and happiness, creating and maintaining a good balance between the pressures of every day and the value of total health.

What is the Plan of StressMap?

This book presents a series of six questionnaires—"maps"—to help you identify the stressors in each area of your life. Here is a sampling of some of the items involved:

- PEOPLE
  Family, friends, marriage, divorce, widowhood, vacations, activities, and giving and receiving of love. Also included are meal preparations, errands, grocery shopping, house repairs, vehicle repairs, housecleaning, laundry, childcare, yardwork, and mending.
- MONEY
  Material goods and possessions, salary, savings, budgets, investments, retirement, bills, and credit.

- **WORK**
  Life's central activity, means of livelihood, and the relationship to the people with whom you work and interact. This area applies to work in or out of the home as well as to schoolwork.
- **BODY**
  Sports, exercise, relaxation, diet, hygiene, medical care, physical surroundings, and life spaces.
- **MIND**
  Formal education, student activities, travel, reading, lectures, educational TV, continuing education, lifelong learning and spirituality.
- **LEISURE**
  Social life, hobbies, cultural activities, creative endeavors, community work, and volunteer organizations.

Mapping the areas of your life that *lead* to stress reactions is not your final goal, of course. Once the stressors are found, you must decide which you are willing to change. We have provided suggestions for modifying your life to reduce your distress. As you progress through this material, you will quickly discover that you can have more control over stress and your reactions to it than you had thought possible.

Even though you will examine each of the six areas of your life separately, you should always keep in mind that these areas are inseparable. Visualize them as working together to create a balanced, positive, *holistic* approach to health!

The six StressMap chapters (3-8) each include a brief introduction and a self-examination. This process of *stressor mapping* is the *first* step in a successful stress management program. The "maps" will help you identify the stressors in your life in six major areas: PEOPLE, MONEY, WORK, LEISURE, MIND, and BODY.

Don't be surprised if you discover that some areas of your life have more stress than others; that's what we hope you *will* learn. This process, involving the six stress maps, is very individual and personal. Even people who live or work closely together will not react to stressors in the same way.

The maps will be useful primarily as a way to *find* your stressors. The second step in stress management is to decide what you want to *do* about them. The Stress Relief and Buffers sections, Chapters 11-20, are designed to help you systematically and inexpensively learn lifelong skills for effective stress management.

Instructions for Following the Six StressMaps:

Answering: Respond to each statement the way you generally feel at this time in your life. Rate every statement by placing a check or "X" in one of the columns. The zero (0) column means "no" or that the statement "does not apply." Columns 1 to 5 indicate "yes," and show how much you are bothered or stressed by the situation. The higher the number you mark, the more stressed you feel.

Scoring: At the end of each map, add up the ratings for each column. For every check mark or "X" in column 5 ("Bothers me a lot"), add 5 points to your score. For every check mark in column 4, add 4 points, and so on. Any response in the zero (0) column receives no points. Enter your score for each area on the composite map on pages 48-49. Follow these same procedures for answering and scoring all six stress maps in Chapters 3-8. P.S. Don't let these instructions stress you—it's really very simple!

3
People StressMap

Relationships with other people are a very complex aspect of life. Are you single, married, widowed, "living together," single-parent, divorced, separated, childless? Relationships include immediate and extended family, such as your partner, spouse, friends, relatives, children, in-laws, grandchildren, acquaintances, and associates.

Consider the endless activities and time involved in the management of relationships, home and living environment: vacations, meals, errands, shopping, cleaning, repairing, doing laundry, caring for the children and/or pets, telephoning, planning, attending social events...Hold it! *Work* is discussed in Chapter 5!

Once again, our point is that a *balance* must be maintained. You are not alone if you find the *activities* of managing your lifestyle tipping the balance and consuming more time than you would like. Relationships depend upon expressing feelings, spending time together, enjoying the company of another, listening, sharing, giving, loving, committing, touching, hugging and communicating. Giving and receiving love are more important than all the "activities" and "duties," tipping the balance back toward intimate relationships of mutual growth and fulfillment.

How are your relationships? Stress with people can make you feel lonely, irritated, frustrated or misunderstood. Sometimes a person can feel overwhelmed and exhausted by the responsibilities, leaving little energy for the loving. Do you find the daily activities and duties creating a burden of pressure on yourself? The set of statements you will now consider is a start in creating a balance in your relationships.

PEOPLE STRESSMAP

	DOES NOT APPLY (NO)	BOTHERS ME A LITTLE				BOTHERS ME A LOT
	0	1	2	3	4	5
1. My children are growing up and leaving home						
2. I recently became separated and/or divorced						
3. Our family needs to spend more time together						
4. I feel at a loss in dealing with my children						
5. I have recently had an addition to the family (birth, adoption)						
6. I have trouble getting along with my relatives						
7. I wish I had a family (spouse or children)						
8. My father has recently died						
9. I am facing the problems associated with elderly parents/relatives						
10. I am always stuck with the job of preparing meals for my family						
11. Too much of my time is spent doing things for others						
12. My mother has recently died						
13. Nobody helps with the repairs needed on the house						

PEOPLE STRESSMAP

14. Child care is my responsibility
15. I wish my family would help more with the laundry
16. I worry that I could be a better parent
17. My relationship with my spouse/partner is deteriorating
18. I have difficulty forming close relationships with (please underline): friends, co-workers, relatives, children, spouse, in-laws,
19. I worry about asking someone for a date
20. I wish I enjoyed sexual intercourse more
21. When I am upset with my spouse/partner, I have difficulty expressing my feelings.
22. I find it difficult to enjoy being out socially with my spouse/partner
23. I tend to deal with my children's problems and questions ineffectively
24. I am prone to lose control when my children misbehave
25. I want my friends to like me because then I will be OK too
26. I like being single, independent, and unattached, but some people think there is something wrong with me

27. I am a widow/widower
28. I like being single, but sometimes I get lonely and think there is something wrong with me
29. I wish people needed me more
30. There is a lack of intimacy/communication with my spouse/partner
31. I tend to refrain from showing feelings of sadness, anger or fear
32. I am a stepparent
33. I have trouble saying "no" to anyone who asks me for something
34. I find it difficult to ask for help
35. I feel I should seek information on parenting
36. It is uncomfortable for me to express feelings of concern, love and warmth for people for whom I care
37. I am a single parent
38. I find it difficult to accept constructive criticism without reacting defensively.
39. I am contemplating divorce.

40. When listening to others, I find myself becoming disinterested and not listening..........
41. I have recently lost a child or close friend through death ....
42. I am contemplating marriage ....
43. I have recently moved and left behind some close friends ....
44. I am experiencing sexual difficulties or frustrations ....
45. I tend to become easily irritated with my co-workers on the job ....

a) Total your score for people stress (you may find it helpful to refer to the instructions for scoring on page 16).
b) If your score is below 25, you are probably dealing effectively with the pressures of people. Congratulations!
c) If your score is between 25 and 75, this is an area you should examine more closely. Your stress level is high enough that you could in the near future experience some physical or mental signs of distress.
d) If your score is over 75, people stress is signaling danger ahead! Please take time now to heed the warning and turn to Chapter 11. There you can reduce your speed and examine the Stress Buffers designed for immediate implementation in the area of *people* stress. Exceeding this level should be a serious warning to you. Don't delay in taking action!

4
Money StressMap

"Money...," according to the song from *Cabaret,* "...makes the world go 'round." Having it, losing it, getting more, paying less...just trying to live with it can make your head go 'round.' One secret to avoiding stress in this area is to accept the almost inevitable fact that the quality of your life depends on having some of it and managing it well. All areas of your life—people, mind, leisure, body, and work—are affected by the presence or absence of money. Material goods and possessions, your career, salary, investments, savings, bills, credit, receipts, income tax and the budget are all associated with the financial area.

Do you see money as a source of happiness or the root of evil? Are finances a topic that will almost inevitably create friction? Is money a means to an end or the end itself? Financial stress can make you feel helpless, frustrated, and angry. It is a major source of marital conflict.

It is possible for money and finances to be a source of happiness (eustress). This next set of questions is a first step in helping you keep the financial aspect of your life in perspective.

MONEY STRESSMAP

	DOES NOT APPLY (NO) 0	BOTHERS ME A LITTLE 1	2	3	4	BOTHERS ME A LOT 5

1. I recently received an increase in my salary/wages.
2. There is a large mortgage on my home.
3. I feel I am barely living from check to check.
4. I recently received an overdue notice for one of my bills.
5. I find myself trying to "keep up with the Joneses"
6. I worry about being able to provide my children with the things they need/want.
7. I or my partner lost a job recently.
8. I have many bills to pay.
9. I or my partner recently began a new job (if yes, mark 5).
10. I seem to buy a lot on credit.
11. I feel financially insecure.
12. I cannot afford the things I would like.

13. *I have difficulty managing a budget* ....

14. *My spouse and/or I retired recently and we have been living on a smaller, fixed income* ....

15. *I am afraid I will fall behind on a mortgage payment or bill* ....

16. *I recently received a cut in salary/wages* ....

17. *The I.R.S. audited me within the last year* ....

18. *My income has been reduced because of a separation, divorce or death* ....

19. *My income is failing more and more to keep up with expenses* ....

20. *I have been delaying a savings or investment program* ....

   a) Total your score for money stress (you may find it helpful to refer to the instructions for scoring on page 16).

   b) If your score is below 13, you are probably dealing effectively with the pressures of money. Congratulations!

   c) If your score is between 13 and 37, this is an area you should examine more closely. Your stress level is high enough that you could in the near future experience some physical or mental signs of distress.

   d) If your score is over 37, money stress is signaling danger ahead! Please take time now to heed the warning and turn to Chapter 12. There you can reduce your speed and examine the Stress Buffers designed for immediate implementation in the area of *money*. Exceeding this level should be a serious warning to you. Don't delay in taking action!

5
Work StressMap

Work stress touches almost everyone: the rodeo cowboy, the nurse, the President of the United States. You do not have to be receiving a salary or working full time to experience it. If you are a student, work part time, or have a career in the home, distress is a possibility.

The "average" worker spends eight hours a day, five days a week, fifty weeks a year on the job. This is an investment (or loss, depending on how you look at it!), of approximately 2,000 hours every year. Since a career is so time-consuming, it may be impossible for some to separate the career from the rest of living. Job literally becomes life, twelve hours a day, evenings and weekends.

How stressful is it for you to deal with work tasks day after day? Do you have deadlines? Do you feel the pressure of having to be competent and successful? How do you react to all those problems that do not have an immediate solution? What are your reactions to professional stressors? Some may feel frustrated, angry, or overwhelmed. Others may try to escape by getting sick, doing busy work that has no relation to the job, or by socializing away the day. Are you the type who fights off the pressures and demands by pushing even harder, working faster and longer? Has work ever been an activity that adds to your general fulfillment and happiness?

Since a means of livelihood can be so different for everyone and can consume so much of each day, you should spend some *extra* time on the following questionnaire, making each item as personal as possible. *This questionnaire is for the eight-to-five factory worker, student, homemaker, non-traditional job-holder, anyone who works! Substitute appropriate words and phrases to fit your situation.*

You may find it hard to accept that your job is a major cause of stress. You may feel that you have no power to change your situation, so why get into it? You may feel you would be more stressed if you were to admit that so much of your time is spent at an activity that is making life progressively more difficult the longer you stay in it. You may feel trapped in a no-win situation; but change is an option. Maybe not a change of careers, but how about all those other changes you can make to create a less stressful job? React to the following list as it relates to your situation. Then be innovative and flexible in your solutions.

WORK STRESSMAP

	DOES NOT APPLY (NO) 0	BOTHERS ME A LITTLE 1	2	3	4	BOTHERS ME A LOT 5

1. Deadlines are a daily part of my job ....
2. I have a problem completing work assignments because of the many interruptions ....
3. I find it necessary to work during some lunches (if yes, mark 5) ....
4. After leaving the job, I generally complete work I have not had time for during the day (if yes, mark 5) ....
5. I find it difficult to work with some of my co-workers ....
6. I need to take some college courses in order to update my skills ....
7. I find it difficult to find meaning in my job ....
8. I find my working environment unpleasant ....
9. I continue to allow myself to accept new job responsibilities without letting go of others ....
10. There is little variety or challenge in my job ....

11. I have recently received a new promotion (if yes, mark 5)
12. I often feel overwhelmed with the demands of my job.
13. My work environment is noisy
14. I feel I should be more satisfied with what I have accomplished at work
15. When I am under pressure I tend to lose my temper.
16. It is difficult to feel comfortable in the presence of my supervisor.
17. I wish there were more closeness among the people with whom I work
18. I would like to feel more confident in my occupation
19. My job is emotionally demanding
20. My work requires extensive preparation and training (if yes, mark 5)
21. I have lost enthusiasm for my job.
22. I have been in the same job for five years or more (if yes, mark 5) *
23. I am caught up in the "busy work" aspects of my job
24. It is hard to look forward to a new life after retirement

WORK STRESSMAP

25. I find it difficult to relax during breaks even when I do take them (if yes, mark 5) ....
26. When I get to work I need more time than I have to prepare for the day ....
27. On my way to and from work, I tend to rehash the problems of the day ....
28. My job is physically demanding ....
29. When starting work projects, I find it difficult to become immediately involved ....
30. My job is at home. I do not get weekends off (if yes, mark 5) ....
31. When hit by questions from all sides, I cannot answer or make a decision ....
32. I am concerned with the goal of being a perfect employee, spouse and parent at the same time ....
33. When I come home from work, I still have the laundry, cooking, shopping, and the cleaning to do ....

34. *Even though I like my work, I feel guilty when I put in extra hours* ....

35. *My job is at home. I cannot walk out and leave it at night*
    (if yes, mark 5) ....

*After about 5 years on a job with no changes in duties, people begin to burn out and not realize it, causing stress in all other areas of life.

a) Total your score for work stress (you may find it helpful to refer to the instructions for scoring on page 16).

b) If your score is below 20, you are probably dealing effectively with the pressures of work. Congratulations!

c) If your score is between 20 and 60, this is an area you should examine more closely. Your stress level is high enough that you could in the near future experience some physical or mental signs of distress.

d) If your score is over 60, work stress is signaling danger ahead! Please take time now to heed the warning and turn to Chapter 13. There you can reduce your speed and examine the Stress Buffers designed for immediate implementation in the area of *work*. Exceeding this level should be a serious warning to you. Don't delay in taking action!

6
Leisure StressMap

"There is a time and a place for leisure activities—after all the work is completed." "Leisure is a luxury of the rich." People who agree with these statements seem to see leisure as a means of reducing stress when it becomes unbearable. But leisure should not be the last resort—the *reaction* to a stressful lifestyle. Ideally, leisure should be a repertoire of activities used regularly to *prevent* life from becoming too stressful.

Do you know what specifically helps you mentally and physically to reduce the effects of stressors? Have you explored social events, hobbies, cultural activities, community involvements and organizational memberships as potential sources of leisure? Do you ever find yourself maintaining a leisure activity even when it becomes a distasteful burden? Which of your leisure activities are free, take only a few minutes of time and are effective?

Stress in the leisure area may result in feelings of guilt or confusion. Some people may feel overwhelmed or frustrated.

The map which follows can help you determine the effectiveness of leisure in your life.

LEISURE STRESSMAP

	DOES NOT APPLY (NO)	BOTHERS ME A LITTLE				BOTHERS ME A LOT
	0	1	2	3	4	5

1. I have very little time for hobbies
2. I have a lot of unfinished projects around the house
3. I would like to spend evenings attending plays, concerts, movies, etc.
4. I spend too much time watching television
5. I wish I spent more time just relaxing and talking with my friends
6. I have put off learning to play a musical instrument
7. I feel I should contribute more of my time to community activities or projects
8. I have put off planting a garden
9. I wish my interests were more varied
10. I should make an attempt to get to know my neighbors
11. I feel I should have a greater number of hobbies and interests

LEISURE STRESSMAP

12. I do two things at once, such as eating while working, reading a magazine while watching TV, etc. (if yes, mark 5) ....
13. I would like to spend more time reading books. ....
14. I would like to participate more in relaxing group or club activities ....
15. When faced with a period of inactivity, it is difficult to occupy myself either mentally or physically (if yes, mark 5) ....
16. I find it difficult to look forward to holidays ....
17. I need a vacation (if yes, mark 5) ....
18. The interior of my home could be more satisfying or pleasing ....
19. I tend to be bored with my life ....

a) Total your score for leisure stress (you may find it helpful to refer to the instructions for scoring on page 16).
b) If your score is below 13, you are probably dealing effectively with the pressures of leisure. Congratulations!
c) If your score is between 13 and 37, this is an area you should examine more closely. Your stress level is high enough that you could in the near future experience some physical or mental signs of distress.
d) If your score is over 37, leisure stress is signaling danger ahead! Please take time now to heed the warning and turn to Chapter 14. There you can reduce your speed and examine the Stress Buffers designed for immediate implementation in the area of *leisure*. Exceeding this level should be a serious warning to you. Don't delay in taking action!

7
Mind StressMap

Your ability to reason, imagine, calculate and verbalize makes you unique. Your mind is a powerful tool you have at your disposal. Do you fully appreciate this tool? Are you developing it to its fullest potential?

Some individuals use their mental powers to memorize large amounts of information or even entire books. Others master several languages. Many receive multiple educational degrees for their knowledge in a number of disciplines. Some develop themselves by reading extensively. All these individuals are not much different from you. The one trait that probably sets them apart is that they have learned that they can control their destinies by what they think. These people have *thought* of themselves as learned, successful, rich, loveable, or anything else—and their intellect, their thoughts, have created the action which led to that reality. What you are now is largely a result of what you think. *You* must take the blame for your own failures...and the credit for your successes.

The mind is also our link to the spirit. In times of distress, crisis or need, many individuals find assistance and comfort in their faith. A belief in God, a supreme being, universal oneness, or whatever is meaningful to you can be a powerful stress reduction technique. Humans all have a spiritual nature, whether or not we subscribe to a particular religious faith. Has your spirituality been a resource in the past, pushed aside in the hustle and bustle of daily activities?

What are you doing, on a regular basis, to develop your unique talents? Have you maintained contact with formal education? Do you gain knowledge by travel? Is reading, both professional and leisure, a regular part of your life? Have you taught yourself how to relax your mind? Are you satisfied with your sleep habits? Can you concentrate? Do you remember what you want? Do you share ideas with others and learn from the ensuing discussion?

Mind stress can lead to confusion and powerlessness. Some become unable to make decisions. Others may feel angry or lonely or frightened when they are unable to think and discuss with confidence. How about you?

MIND STRESSMAP

	DOES NOT APPLY (NO)	BOTHERS ME A LITTLE				BOTHERS ME A LOT
	0	1	2	3	4	5

1. I find it difficult to feel any fulfillment or joy in religion
2. I need to read self-help books (if yes, mark 5)*
3. I find it difficult to adjust to personal problems
4. I have reviewed my lifetime values at least once in the past year (if no, mark 5)
5. I try not to cry
6. I wish I knew how to change my feelings
7. Sometimes I feel I ought to believe in God
8. I find it difficult to set limits for myself or stick to them
9. I need to feel more enthusiastic about life
10. I wish I read more books for pleasure
11. I wish I felt more worthwhile and important as a person
12. I am afraid of losing my faith in God

MIND STRESSMAP

13. I would like to spend more time reading magazines or newspapers
14. I would like to watch more educational programs on television
15. I wish I felt a oneness or unity with others or the environment
16. I daydream or fall asleep during lectures, seminars, classes, etc.
17. Little things irritate me
18. I want to believe in God but find it difficult to develop this belief
19. I have poor concentration
20. I find it difficult to remember things
21. I feel restless
22. I would like my life to have more meaning and purpose
23. I want to feel more satisfied with myself and others
24. I feel the need for religion but it is difficult to find what I want in any one church
25. I feel out of control at times
26. I find myself being apathetic

27. I wish I had a personal relationship with God
28. I have felt discrimination and/or harrassment (physical, sexual, age)
29. I need to enjoy my life more
30. I want to strengthen my spiritual beliefs
31. I find it difficult to laugh
32. I would like my belief in God to give me more energy, motivation, fulfillment and happiness
33. I would like to find and use ways to relax my mind
34. I am depressed
35. Sometimes I feel that religion is necessary and sometimes I doubt its value
36. I have nightmares
37. I tend to be easily startled by small sounds
38. Getting old bothers me

*Self responsibility in the form of developmental reading is a key to personal stress management. No outside, self-help reading limits a person's resources.

MIND STRESSMAP

a) Total your score for mind stress (you may find it helpful to refer to the instructions for scoring on page 16).

b) If your score is below 20, you are probably dealing effectively with the pressures of mind stress. Congratulations!

c) If your score is between 20 and 60, this is an area you should examine more closely. Your stress level is high enough that you could in the near future experience some physical or mental signs of distress.

d) If your score is over 60, mind stress is signaling danger ahead! Please take time now to heed the warning and turn to Chapter 15. There you can reduce your speed and examine the Stress Buffers designed for immediate implementation in the area of *mind* stress. Exceeding this level should be a serious warning to you. Don't delay in taking action!

Frank and Ernest

8
Body StressMap

"Why should I push my body even more by playing racketball?"

"I'm running enough, I don't need to jog!"

"I'm not bedridden, why should I see a doctor?"

"I watch my diet; I'm not overweight...that much."

"Relax? Sure, I relax when I finally get to sleep."

"One of these days I'll have the office and home that I've always dreamed about. Until then, I can survive with a little confusion."

Do you ever find yourself making some or all of these statements? If you do, then you may be ignoring one of your most valuable resources—your body and its health.

The connection is simple yet incredibly important: When your physical well-being is neglected or abused, your overall performance is threatened. If you experience physical stress, you may feel tired, sluggish or unmotivated. Some people start experiencing more illnesses; others resort to alcohol, cigarettes or more caffeine to reduce tension, or simply become edgy and irritable.

Do you believe that physical conditioning is a *luxury*? Do you say to yourself that you don't have *time* to think about sports, exercise, relaxation, diet, hygiene, medical care, physical surroundings and life spaces? Do you tell yourself that you can life without all the health "fads" going around? Have you ever considered how much you could be shortening your life by short-changing your physical well-being? The following stressmap may give you a different perspective.

BODY STRESSMAP

	DOES NOT APPLY (NO) 0	ABOUT ONCE A MONTH 1	ABOUT ONCE A WEEK 2	ABOUT TWICE A WEEK 3	DAILY 4	ALMOST ALL THE TIME 5
1. I have had difficulties maintaining my correct weight						
2. I have not had three consecutive weeks of vacation each year (if true, mark 5)						
3. Within the last year I have experienced the following:						
a. Muscle tightness or aching in the back						
b. Tightly gripping a chair, steering wheel, clenching fists, etc.						
c. Cold or clammy hands						
d. Muscle tightness or aching in the shoulders						
e. Frowning						
f. Squinting						
g. Clenching teeth, aching in the jaw						
h. Bruxism (grinding teeth during the day or at night)						
i. Frequent headaches/migraines						

STRESSMAP

j. Stroke (if yes, mark 5) ....
k. Stuttering ....
l. Fainting spells ....
4. I seem to have lots of colds/viruses/infections ....
5. More and more I have needed medical care ....
6. I feel anxious, nervous, jittery, jumpy ....
7. I feel I am accident prone ....
8. I use the following:
   a. Aspirin ....
   b. Tranquilizers ....
   c. Pain killers ....
   d. Sleeping aids ....
9. I am exposed to the following in my environment:
   a. Noise ....
   b. Extreme changes in temperature ....
   c. Vibrations ....

BODY STRESSMAP

d. Air pollutants (dust, smoke, strong odors, chemical vapors, etc.) ....

10. I have acquired a disability within the last year (if true, mark 5) ....

11. Within the last year I have experienced the following:

   a. Muscle tightness or aching in the back ....
   b. Muscle tightness or aching in the chest ....
   c. Heart attack (if true, mark 5) ....
   d. High blood pressure (hypertension) (if true, mark 5) ....
   e. Short, irregular or shallow breathing ....
   f. Heart racing or pounding ....

12. I have trouble falling asleep ....

13. I prefer to ride an elevator than climb stairs (if true, mark 5) ....

14. My daily activities do not include moderate physical activity such as rearing young children, mowing the lawn, standing all day (if yes, mark 5) ....

15. Within the last year I have experienced the following:

   a. Loss of appetite ....

b. Muscle tightness or aching in the abdomen
c. Feeling nauseous during a crisis
d. Churning in the stomach
e. Diarrhea
f. Constipation
g. Ulcers (if true, mark 5)
h. Spastic colon (if true, mark 5)
i. Gastritis (if true, mark 5)

16. When I do take a vacation, I find that I have a hard time relaxing or enjoying myself (if true, mark 5)

17. I eat refined (table) sugar

18. Within the last year I have experienced the following:

a. Nervous perspiration
b. Muscle tightness or aching in the legs
c. Finding my whole body becoming stiff and tight as I go through the day

BODY STRESSMAP

d. Loss of energy/chronic fatigue ....

e. Nervous habits (nail biting, neck rubbing, foot tapping, jerky movements, etc.). ....

f. Waking up during the night for no apparent reason ....

19. I drink two or more cups of coffee or tea per day (do not count herbal teas or decaffeinated coffees) (if true, mark 5) ....

20. I do not engage in some form of enjoyable strenuous exercise for a minimum of 15 min. at least three times per week (if true, mark 5). ....

21. I have three or more alcoholic drinks per week* ....

22. I smoke cigarettes, pipes, cigars, etc. ....

23. Within the last year I have experienced the following:

a. Diabetes (if true, mark 5) ....

b. Cancer (if true, mark 5) ....

c. Arthritis (if true, mark 5) ....

d. Rashes ....

e. Allergies (if true, mark 5) ....

24. *I add salt to my food during cooking and at the table*
    (if yes, mark 5) ....

25. *When I exercise I skip the ten minutes of warm up stretching and the ten minutes of cool down activities (if yes, mark 5)* ....

26. *I eat chocolate of some type* ....

27. *I rarely use rapid-releasing techniques to deal with stress (deep muscle relaxation, meditation, imagery, body scanning) (if true, mark 5)* ..

*Alcohol, in small amounts, is usually not harmful and, under a physician's direction, can even be helpful in certain situations. However, if alcohol is one of your primary sources of relaxation, reevaluate your stress level and stress relief techniques.

a) Total your score for body stress (you may find it helpful to refer to the instructions for scoring on page 16).

b) If your score is below 37, you are probably dealing effectively with the pressures of body stress. Congratulations!

c) If your score is between 37 and 112, this is an area you should examine more closely. Your stress level is high enough that you could in the near future experience some physical or mental signs of distress.

d) If your score is over 112, body stress is signaling danger ahead! Please take time now to heed the warning and turn to Chapter 16. There you can reduce your speed and examine the Stress Buffers designed for immediate implementation in the area of *body* stress. Exceeding this level should be a serious warning to you. Don't delay in taking action!

9
Your Life StressMap

It's done! You have six completed StressMaps, and your scores are plotted on the next page, "Your Life StressMap."

No doubt about it, responding to all those statements involved hard work and thoughtful self-analysis—and perhaps even a little stress! Now you are ready to review them and find out some important information about your pressure points. The time you spend on this chapter will pay off later in the book, where you will follow a stress *relief* plan to effectively cope with the life stress you identify here.

But first, your Life StressMap. Your stress is a unique combination of pressures. As you review each of your six StressMaps, you'll benefit most from identifying *patterns* of stress and applying stress management techniques. This approach will reduce or eliminate several stressors, which in turn will reduce other related stressors.

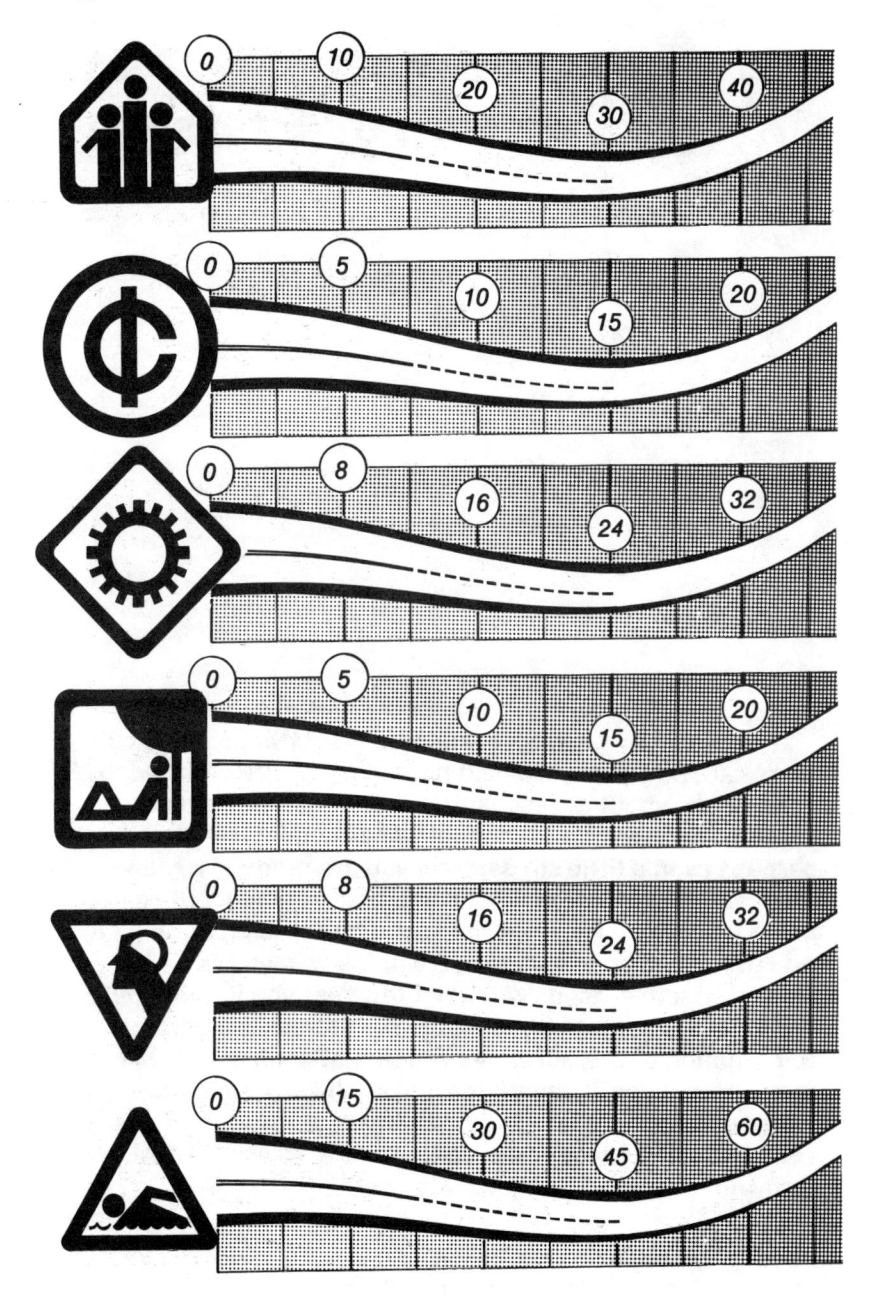

STRESSMAP

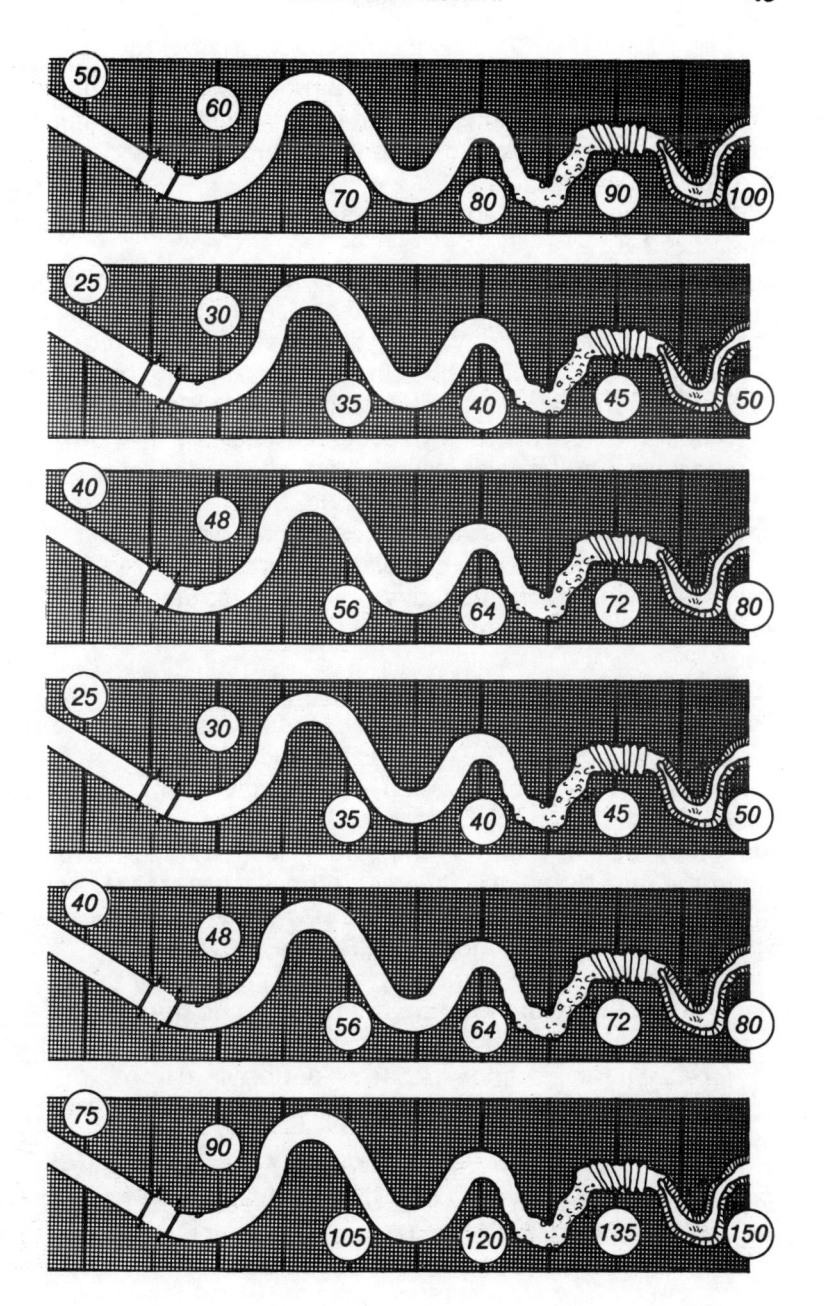

YOUR LIFE STRESSMAP 49

Your stress built up over time as a runaway vehicle builds up speed going downhill. The goal in stress management is to begin a chain reaction to bring your "runaway" under control.
1. Be sure you have mapped your six scores for stress from Chapters 3-8.
2. Look at the stress levels for each area and identify the two or three areas which have the highest stress. List them on the top (section A) of the "Stress Management Planning Worksheet" that follows these instructions on pages 54-55.
3. Examine the *sample* "Stress Management Planning Worksheet." Note especially section B, "Patterns." The person shown in the sample worksheet had highest stress in the area of *Work*. With too much to do, there was no time for fun and relaxation. This was reflected in the next highest stress area: *Leisure.* With no balanced recreation, play or tension-releasing activities, physical problems started surfacing. The result was the third highest stress level: *Body.*

Stress in one area gradually creeps into other areas. Eventually, if not relieved, high levels of stress may develop in all six areas of life. The result is holistic *distress.*

No matter what your situation, you are never beyond hope. Whether only one StressMap is high or all six are off the scale, you can still find relief. Carefully reading the signs along the road to stress is the beginning of stress relief. On the highway, you must heed the signs which say "Reduce Speed Ahead" or "Danger, Road Blocked." Your StressMap scores are *your* own personal signs. Read them well, understand what they are telling you, and then start doing something specific about stress in your life.

Here are a few common life stress patterns we have observed in our work with hundreds of stress management trainees:

- *The Social Butterfly:* Charlene has without a doubt the most active social calendar in town. President of the PTA, she also belongs to the Garden Club, the Community Beautification Society, the First Church Women's Circle, the

# Sample Stress Management Planning Worksheet

A. HIGHEST STRESS LEVELS	B. PATTERNS
1. work 2. leisure 3. body	Always behind & rushed at work. Less & less time for leisure (self, family, friends). Physical problems.

C. STRESSOR STATEMENTS	D. PRIORITY GROUP	E. WHO, WHEN, WHERE?	F. GENERAL STRESS MANAGEMENT GOALS AND NOTES
- I do not engage in some form of strenuous exercise for a minimum of 15 mins. at least 3 times a week	2	Who? I am responsible for my own stress. When? Everyday almost on a continuous basis. Where? My stress began on the job, but quickly overflowed to home life.	- Improve my time management. - Get medical help for my nervousness. - Learn how to relax at work. - Get help with home chores. - Notes: relaxation time management
- I feel anxious, nervous, jittery, jumpy	1		
- I feel my heart racing or pounding daily	3		
- I cannot set limits for myself or stick to them	4		
- I have frequent headaches	3		
- More and more I find I need medical care	1		
- When I get to work, I find I need more time	2		

YOUR LIFE STRESSMAP

County Republicrat Central Committee, and several more groups. She barely sees her family, has not read a book in months, and lives by the clock and calendar.
- *The Workaholic:* Fred owns and manages his own business. He has remained successful even in hard economic times by "pure determination and hard work." In the office by 7 a.m., he always takes a briefcase of work home, and spends most evenings at his home computer working out sales projections and financial reports.
- *The Hobby Horse:* Lorraine has worked with wood since she was a small child watching her grandfather turn out spool beds and chairs on his lathe. She now creates hundreds of small and large objects from wood, carving and shaping for hours, literally forgetting time and other activities. She worries that shortages of fine carving woods will create difficulties for her future projects.
- *The StressEater:* Howard doesn't enjoy eating; he eats compulsively from habit, boredom, anxiety, even addiction. His food habits center on popular "junk foods," and he abhors anything which has been called "healthy." A chain smoker as well, Howard does not really taste his food, but tends to eat as a ritual.
- *The Winner:* Joe is a runner. About four years ago, he took up jogging because of its popularity and apparent health value. As he developed strength and capacity to run, he increased his daily jog to twice a day, and gradually doubled his speed. He joined a running club, and entered club contests, working his way up to the annual 26-mile marathon. Last year he won the local event, and this year entered the New York marathon, finishing 103rd in a field of thousands. He now trains six hours each day...

Do any of these life stress patterns remind you of people you know—yourself perhaps?

4. *Write* a brief note about the patterns you see in your own stress. Use section B of your own "Stress Management Planning Worksheet."

5. Go back through each of your six area StressMaps in Chapters 3 through 8. In section C of the "Stress

Management Planning Worksheet," list *every* statement from all six StressMaps that you rated with a "5." (Section C is the first column of the worksheet.) If you need more space, continue on another piece of paper. If you don't have at least 10 statements you rated "5," go back and list every statement you rated with a "4" also.

6. Review all the stressor statements you have listed and group them according to their levels of stress. Which statements are most stressful, annoying or bothersome? Which would you like to eliminate immediately? Mark these statements with a "1" in section D of the worksheet ("Priority Group").

Choose the next most stressful items and rate them with a "2." Continue until you have assigned *all* your 4 and/or 5 stressor statements to a priority group.

Take your time with this step.

7. Concentrate on the rankings you gave to your stressors in step 6. What patterns do you see? Make a note in the third (section E) column as to:
- *Who* is involved (yourself, spouse, co-worker)
- *When* the stressor occurs (continuously, mornings, on weekends)
- *Where* the stressor is found (on the job, in school, at home)

The person in the sample worksheet discovered that she was the main person responsible for her own high stress levels. Stress occurred daily, almost continuously on the job but overflowed into all other areas.

8. As you review your own patterns in detail, pay special attention to several areas of your life experiences which may contribute to your capacity to deal with stress: relaxation; physical activity; eating habits; assertiveness; and time management. We will have more to say about these subjects in later chapters. For now, make a special note in the last column (section F) of any patterns you see which are related to them.

Stress Management Planning Worksheet

A. HIGHEST STRESS LEVELS	

C. STRESSOR STATEMENTS	D. PRIORITY GROUP

YOUR LIFE STRESSMAP

B. PATTERNS

E. WHO, WHEN, WHERE?	F. GENERAL STRESS MANAGEMENT GOALS AND NOTES

9. Finally, review your stressors, priorities, patterns, and notes. What would you like to do about them? Write a few statements of "general goals" in section F. (In the next chapter, we'll discuss how to convert these *general* goals into achievable steps.)

Any time you want to follow a map, you must first find out where you are. Only then can you chart a course to your desired destination. You have just completed that step. Now you know where you are and you have a better understanding about your own stress patterns and how they are related to each other. You also know the "who, when, and where" of your stress. And you have established some general goals for change. Using this knowledge to chart a specific course to less stress is the next step.

Eek and Meek

10
Life Stress Planning

Relief is on the way! The remaining chapters in this book could be among the most important reading of your life. Proceed carefully!

At this point you have some important information about your Life StressMap. You know which of the six StressMaps are the most distressful. You also know the major people, places and times involved in your stress. Now for the road to stress relief.

Your Life StressMap is one-of-a-kind; stress itself is very personalized, reflecting your lifestyle. In the same way, a stress relief plan must be designed to fit your unique needs. While no two relief plans are exactly alike, each, if it is to be effective, should incorporate these five basic stress relief skills:

1. *Relaxation* creates changes in your body that reverse the effects of distress. You need the ability to relax your body, anywhere, when you begin to feel tension and pressure. Without this skill, stress gradually builds over weeks and months until something drastic happens which *forces* a slowing down. Relaxation is a free, quick, calming, and refreshing activity—the alternative to physical and psychological difficulties and the bills, helplessness, and anguish that usually accompany them. Chapter 17 will teach you specific skills in how to relax.

2. *Eating habits* directly contribute to stress. In many ways, "your stress is what you eat." Stress relief through nutrition is not severe fasting, complete abstinence from everything commercial, or expensive health foods. We advocate an understanding of nutritional basics and a common sense approach to your eating habits. We also urge a gradual change of eating habits as you adapt and learn more about what you put in your body. We suggest that you make eating a part of your overall program of stress management while you make it an adventure in discovery. Chapter 18 begins the adventure.

3. *Physical activity* is play. Play for a child, you may remember, is pure enjoyment, with freedom and exhilaration mixed in. Finding your own play activities and letting yourself enjoy them regularly is a powerful mental and physical stress relief. Chapter 19 is a start to finding your play.

4. *Time management* is a useful tool to keep time from controlling and terrorizing you and adding more stress. Satisfaction, accomplishment, peace of mind, and control can result when you hone your time management skills to produce stress relief. Chapter 20 gives some tips.

5. *Assertiveness* contributes to control of your life without causing you stress or creating it in others. Effective self-assertion is another very important skill to develop. Stress relief depends in part on being assertive—able to express yourself and your needs without pushing others around.

Your next step is to decide how you will *adapt* these general stress management techniques to fit your individual situation. As you develop plans, you must be sure that you *want* to work on them and that you can *realistically* accomplish them. Every goal must also be stated very carefully in *specific* terms. Examples:

Unacceptable goal: I will try to relax more.
Acceptable goal: I will go to my quiet place every evening for 20 minutes and listen to my *Seapeace* album.

Unacceptable goal: I will improve my time management skills.

Acceptable goal: I will purchase *How to Get Control of Your Time and Your Life* and begin by reading one chapter every night. I will set a small goal after each chapter to practice a technique.

Look at the sample "Stress Management Plan." The stress management program for this individual would require approximately three hours each week to gain better control. Gaining better control over the workload will produce more leisure time which, carefully used, will result in a healthier body.

Sample Stress Management Plan

A. GENERAL GOALS AND AREAS OF NOTE	B. PRIORITY GROUP	C. SPECIFIC STRESS MANAGEMENT PLANS
- Improve my time management.	2	**Time Management** 1 - Make better work plans every morning 2 - Delegate at work & at home 3 - Evaluate time & energy for any new project
- Get medical help for my nervousness.	1	
- Get help with home chores	3	
- Notes: relaxation, time mgt.		**Relaxation** 1 - Do neck-stretching exercises every hour at work 2 - Do 15 min relaxing exercise at lunch. **Physical Fitness** 1 - Start Jazzercise 2 - Take 5 min. walk at lunchtime

Now refer back to your "Stress Management Planning Worksheet" on pages 54 and 55. In section F, you wrote some general goals for yourself. This is the time to translate those general goals into specific, acceptable terms. Use the Stress Management Plan on page 60 and 61, the procedures

Stress Management Plan

A. GENERAL GOALS AND AREAS OF NOTE [from Chapter 9]	B. PRIORITY GROUP

C. SPECIFIC STRESS MANAGEMENT PLANS

noted above, and the sample Stress Management Plan as guides. Add goals you did not identify in Chapter 9, but be sure to make them very specific at this time. You are developing a plan for *action* now, and it must be made up of steps you *can* accomplish!

As you think about your own goals, it will help to examine the "Stress Buffers" chapters for ideas and leads. Become a real Sherlock Holmes: one of the ideas in a chapter may lead to a book which may be the key to helping you cope with a stress pattern. Take a little extra time to investigate thoroughly; you owe it to yourself!

Stress management skills, like eating and sleeping, are necessities of life. You need them all on a *regular* basis to remain healthy. You undoubtedly have modified your eating and sleeping habits at different points in your life to fit your changing needs. The same should be true for stress management techniques. They must become a permanent part of your lifestyle if you are to achieve and maintain high level wellness and eustressful living.

Enjoy yourself as you design your own stress relief program, and commit it to writing by using the "Stress Management Plan" format provided here.

It takes courage to let go of stress, and it can be scary to take control of your life. That's what the remainder of this book offers: control through stress relief. In many ways changing your life begins with being assertive with yourself. Decide to *follow* your plan, and start your adventure in stress relief.

The next six chapters offer "Stress Buffers"—short-term suggestions for immediate response to the six areas of life stress you have mapped. They will help you over immediate day-to-day stress hurdles.

Chapters 17 to 20 provide greater depth of assistance with the five major stress relief areas we have identified: relaxation, physical activity, eating habits, assertiveness and time management.

Have you completed your personal Stress Management Plan? Your *next* step is to begin to put it into practice!

11

People Stress Buffers

Stress-Buffers SUGGESTIONS NOTES IDEAS TIPS RESOURCES SHARING POTPOURRI

FAMILY COUNCILS   Once-a-week meetings for the whole family provide a special opportunity to discuss those situations which are going to cause some changes or decisions to be made for the whole family. Items for discussion might include household chores, vacation plans, budgeting, etc. Anyone over six years of age would be expected to share in the participation. This meeting should not deteriorate into a "gripe" or "preaching" session, but should provide an opportunity to express oneself and experience a democracy. A book has been published describing this process: *Family Council* by Dr. Rudolph Dreikurs, Shirley Gould and Dr. Raymond Corsini.

MEALS   Meals too can be a family time, not just additional television time. Meals provide the only time when the entire family is together at the same time. Thus the emphasis should be placed on increasing the pleasantness and the quality of this time. Make meals a time when everyone can share positive experiences of the day.

SMILE   Analyze what makes you smile, and make a real effort to smile more often. Maybe it is a Peter Sellers movie, an article by Erma Bombeck, or a comic strip. Take the time to help yourself smile.

CHILDREN & BEHAVIOR No children are perfect; there are times when they actually misbehave! In dealing with children, and making parent survival easier, you might want to consider the following thoughts.

- Parents and children should share mutual respect; neither adult nor child should take advantage of one another.
- A child is nurtured by encouragement just as a plant is by water.
- Punishment should be based on natural consequences. A child needs to be "protected" from these consequences only in times of danger. Obviously you won't allow a child to experience the "natural consequences" of running into a busy street or playing with matches.
- When your words fail to gain the response you want from your child, take action. Remember your child can tune you out just as well as you can tune out the child. Base your conversations with your child on friendliness, and do not discipline with verbal threats. Do not try to converse in times of conflict. It is inevitable that you will say or do something you will later regret. Perhaps withdrawing from the scene of conflict is the most effective action.
- Forego trying to create a dependent child. Encourage the child to develop his/her own abilities. It might take more time, but the child will learn to be more responsible.
- Try to understand the reason behind your child's misbehavior. Remember that the child is trying to gain social status, even though the child's goals may be misdirected (attention getting, power, revenge or display of inadequacy).

PARENTING/STEPPARENTING SKILLS Another avenue for consideration is updating or acquiring more appropriate parenting skills. It is a foregone conclusion that no one ever teaches us to be parents, so there should be no embarrassment in claiming ignorance.

Many community colleges offer "parent effectiveness"

courses. You might also consider acquiring a book describing exceptional parenting skills. Good books include: *Systematic Training for Effective Parenting* and *Raising a Responsible Child* by Dr. Don Dinkmeyer and Gary D. McKay.

VACATION   At one of the family councils, combine efforts to decide on a vacation site that everyone can enjoy. Be sure that each family member can have his/her share in the decision-making process.

HOBBIES/INTERESTS   If you find yourself dissatisfied with life in general, it may be time to develop some new interests/hobbies or perhaps something as risky as a career change or a return to school for further training.

DIVORCE/SEPARATION   The crisis of divorce or separation brings about new and frightening circumstances in your life which forces you into new routines, new behaviors, and a lot of stress. Many community organizations, such as churches and colleges, sponsor groups dealing with emotions involved in this grieving process. Another resource would be books such as *Creative Divorce* by Mel Krantzler and *Rebuilding* by Bruce Fisher.

PEOPLE   Everyone needs a confidante or a good friend. Cultivate or rekindle such a relationship, and risk sharing your emotions and feelings. You will most likely find the risk worthwhile.

GRIEVING   If there has been a recent loss of someone important to you, consider joining a group to help you deal with your feelings. Also, you might find helpful some books by Elisabeth Kubler-Ross: *On Death and Dying* and *Death: The Final Stage of Growth*.

REPAIRS Consider repairing a car, a radio, a piece of furniture or other items with a friend, and you will find that the companionship is as rewarding as the new skill you may learn.

COOKING Call up a friend each week, and ask him or her for a favorite recipe; then try it!

TELEVISION If you find that you are spending too much time in front of the television, consider moving it to a less accessible location in the house. Visit your local library and check out some "best sellers" and place them in strategic reading locations like the bedroom and bathroom. The chapter on Leisure has a few other ideas on the television.

ASSERTION Learn responsible assertive behavior which will allow you to increase your personal effectiveness. Being assertive means standing up for your personal rights and expressing your feelings, thoughts, and opinions in a direct, honest, and appropriate way which does not violate another's personal rights. Many colleges offer short courses on assertiveness training. If you prefer, just get involved in some reading on the subject. Some good books to try are *Asserting Yourself, Don't Say Yes When You Want to Say No,* and *Your Perfect Right: A Guide to Assertive Living.*

HOUSEHOLD DUTIES Try some new ideas for some monotonous everyday chores. Enroll in a cooking class for some new recipes, or check out some cookbooks from the public library. Set aside one day a week (or at least one night a week) just for fun. The chapter on Leisure has some good suggestions. Try car pooling or riding a bike to work. The Leisure chapter has some ideas on rewards that would also apply here.

NEW WAYS TO BE FRIENDS AND LOVERS

- Purchase five or six romantic greeting cards all at once. Write special thoughts and leave them in a different place every week or so.
- Spread a blanket in the living room. Have a wine, cheese, and fruit picnic while listening to your favorite music. Forget about the time and concentrate on who is with you.
- When that special one is working intensely for long hours, give him or her a loving two-minute neck and shoulder massage.
- Have supper prepared when she/he walks in the door. This is especially appreciated when it is not your scheduled night to cook.
- Plan a small (or big) "YOU ARE LOVED" party. Invite your friend or lover's special friends. Have each bring his/her favorite verse or poem which expresses a special feeling.
- Rekindle a relationship by planning a quiet evening where the two of you share memories, photos or old letters from your relationship.
- Make a list of all the strengths and positive points you see and like in your special one. Write three or four at a time on small notes and leave them in different spots at different but regular intervals. Say it simply such as: "I like you because you are (list the strengths). To be continued...."
- Save a little money here and there until you have enough to give your special one the cash to spend only on him or herself.
- Spend an evening lying on a blanket watching for shooting stars while sipping a favorite drink.
- Offer to do the laundry, lawn, shopping or any other chore if he/she uses the extra time to relax.
- Enroll both of you in an activity you both enjoy or would like to learn (dancing, ceramics, wine tasting, gourmet cooking, stained glass, exercise...).
- Buy a plant or flower arrangement. It will mean even more if it is not for a special occasion. (Many men find this especially meaningful!)

- Buy an album of relaxing special effects, like ocean waves or a forest stream. Have a living room picnic with the background sounds.
- Set aside an hour on a regular basis (at least once a week) to share memories, experiences, thoughts, dreams, ideas. Sometimes it helps to preselect the topic.
- Give a body massage by candlelight using incense, lotions, body paints, vibrators, or whatever else pleases. Make a massage a *regular* happening.
- Do tasks or chores together. Talk while you are working. It's amazing how enjoyable work can become and how fast it seems to get done.
- Select a theme such as vacations, your future together, a special occasion from your past, a shared dream, dating mementos. Collect photos, magazine pictures, and quotes. Spend an hour or two a month making a collage together.
- Pick a weekend or even a full week and switch chores around the house. Talk about how it felt over a relaxing meal.
- Before the weekends arrive, spend a few minutes together planning some special time together. This is especially important if one or both of you have a tendency to work away the weekend.

You should have the idea now! Be creative; dream up your own thoughtful and fun ways to increase your friendship or deepen your love, depending on your relationship.

People Bibliography

Alberti, Robert and Emmons, Michael, *Your Perfect Right: A Guide to Assertive Living*

Bach, George and Wyden, Peter, *The Intimate Enemy: How to Fight Fair in Love and Marriage*

Bach, George and Deutsch, Ronald, *Pairing*

Bartz, Wayne and Rasor, Richard, *Surviving with Kids: A Lifeline for Overwhelmed Parents*

Bower, Sharon and Gordon, *Asserting Yourself: A Practical Guide for Positive Change*

Cheek, Donald K., *Assertive Black...Puzzled White*

Dinkmeyer, Don and McKay, Gary, *Raising a Responsible Child*

Dreikurs, Rudolf, Gould, Shirley and Corsini, Raymond, *Family Council*

Fensterheim, Herbert and Baer, Jean, *Don't Say Yes When You Want to Say No*

Fisher, Bruce, *Rebuilding: When Your Relationship Ends*

Frankl, Victor, *Man's Search for Meaning*

Gordon, Thomas, *Parent Effectiveness Training*

Gregg, Elizabeth and Boston Children's Medical Center Staff, *What to Do When There's Nothing to Do*

Johnson, June, *838 Ways to Amuse a Child*

Krantzler, Mel, *Creative Divorce*

Kubler-Ross, Elisabeth, *Death: The Final Stage of Growth*

Kubler-Ross, Elisabeth, *On Death and Dying*

Kuzma, Kay, *Prime-Time Parenting*

Lange, Arthur and Jakubowski, Patricia, *Responsible Assertive Behavior*

Powell, John, *The Secret of Staying in Love*

Powell, John, *Why Am I Afraid to Love?*

Rogers, Carl, *Becoming Partners: Marriage and Its Alternatives*

12
Money Stress Buffers

Stress-Buffers **SUGGESTIONS NOTES** IDEAS **TIPS** RESOURCES **SHARING** POTPOURRI

CHILDREN   Begin early to help your children experience money management in order to build a firm foundation concerning money values. Some experiences you might create for youngsters include:
- opening a savings account
- preparing a grocery shopping list
- developing a plan for earning money
- doing comparative shopping
- allowances
- contributing to church and/or charities
- developing a spending plan

FOOD   Develop a family food plan which compares economical, low-cost, moderate-cost and liberal plans. The U.S. Department of Agriculture has many suggestions (Washington, DC 20250). Ask them for a list of their pamphlets.

MEDICAL   Medical expenses often snow people under and place them in desperate situations in times of crisis. In order to reduce the prolonged effect, consider the following ideas:
- Secure a family physician while you are well, and therefore have an opportunity to do some comparative shopping before the *need* arises.
- If a stay in the hospital is inevitable, do without a private room. Also, talk over with your doctor the possibility of

choosing the hospital. There are often differences in hospital charges.
- If you receive a prescription, speak to your druggist about a "generic" brand.
- Be sure your medical insurance is updated before you need to use it.
- Don't forget that medical expenses are tax deductions, so keep records.

MORE ON BUDGET   Consider working out a "crash" budget so that you are ready if you ever reach a financial crisis. Many community organizations offer money management counseling: labor unions, credit unions, family service agencies, adult education classes and county extension home economists. When beginning your financial planning, be sure you have clear-cut goals that will incorporate your particular goals and values.

EMOTIONAL OUTLETS   Emotions play a large part in the waste of money. Comments like "nothing is too good for my kids" and "whenever I am depressed, I go shopping" lead to trouble and overspending.

MAINTAIN   "Do it yourself" and "tune-up" classes are probably available in your community and can save you when it comes to costly maintenance for the family vehicle. Similar opportunities exist in home landscaping, furniture refinishing, small appliance repair, clothing construction and more.

BUDGET   It does not matter if you are just making it from payday to payday or already have your dream income—a budget is a must. Many communities have free consumer credit counseling services for anyone who wants to set up a budget or get a better handle on the bills. They teach you how to budget and coordinate a repayment schedule with all your creditors.

Most bookstores have workbooks on the basics of financial budgeting. The federal government has a pamphlet for less than $2.00: *A Guide to Budgeting for the Family.*

RAISES If you have a workable budget and then get a raise, consider having part of all of the difference automatically sent to a savings account or credit union. It is an excellent way to start and then continue a savings program—*before* you get used to having the extra money!

FREEBIES If you are looking for free information, read the *Consumer Information Catalog* published by the federal government. Write to: The Consumer Information Center, Pueblo, CO 81009. You can get something for nothing!! Try the *Consumers' Resource Handbook* (Cat. No. 635H) which offers helpful guidelines for dealing with complaints concerning consumer problems, *National Consumer Buying Alert* (Cat. No. 624H)—great for comparative buying—and *Gasoline: More Miles per Gallon* (Cat. No. 513H).

POTPOURRI
- IDEA: Check out the *wealth* of books, magazines, articles, seminars and TV programs on everything possible that will help you get ahead financially.
- IDEA: Have a "home energy efficiency audit." Your local public utilities service probably offers it. Then do the recommended upgrading yourself.
- IDEA: Try car pooling or leaving one car at home a day or two a week.
- IDEA: Offer a small reward to the children for turning out the lights consistently when they leave a room.
- IDEA: Share day care and/or babysitting with friends or neighbors. Do not exchange money, but devise an equitable system for trading child care time and services. Make sure you have a good agreement with all involved.
- IDEA: Encourage the children to seek jobs so they can help out with a few of their own needs or wants.

- IDEA: Try making items for gifts. You can't help stumbling across ideas in the popular magazines. Do it as a family, and save money in the process.
- IDEA: Have a *regular* garage sale.
- IDEAS: Shop for quality instead of for quantity. You will save money in the long run. Read up on the products in consumer rating publications (found in almost all libraries) *before* purchasing. Do not buy on impulse. Shop around, compare, wait for sales.
- IDEA: Set up a bartering system with friends and neighbors and share knowledge, skills, and services.
- IDEA: Save and plan ahead for good investments: real estate, gold and silver, precious gems, oriental rugs and furniture, American Indian rugs and pottery, antiques, art objects, stamp collections.

Money Bibliography

Chadwick, Janet, *How to Live on Almost Nothing and Have Plenty*
Consumer Union of the U.S., *Consumer Reports*
Goldbeck, Nikki and David, *The Supermarket Handbook: Access to Whole Foods*
Hartwig, Daphne M., *Make Your Own Groceries*
Hill, Napoleon, *Think and Grow Rich*
Jones, Peter, *How to Cut Heating and Cooling Costs*
Mandino, Og, *The Greatest Salesman in the World*
Porter, Sylvia, *Sylvia Porter's New Money Book for the 80's*
Quinn, Jane Bryant, *Everyone's Money Book*
Ruff, Howard, *How to Prosper During the Coming Bad Years*
Schlayer, Mary and Cooley, Marilyn, *How to Be a Financially Secure Woman*
U.S. Government Printing Office, *A Guide to Budgeting for the Family* (S/N 001-000-03514-2)
U.S. Government Printing Office, *How to Buy Food* (S/N 001-016-00090-3)
Wolfe, Ralph and Clegg, Peter, *Home Energy for the Eighties*

13

Work Stress Buffers

Stress-Buffers SUGGESTIONS
NOTES IDEAS TIPS RESOURCES
SHARING POTPOURRI

RELATIONSHIPS Make an effort to seek out colleagues and form rewarding, pleasant, and cooperative relationships. (Review Chapter 11 for ideas.)

PRIORITIES Be realistic about *how much* you can handle on the job and learn to manage the priorities. A good reference is Lakein's *How to Get Control of Your Time and Your Life,* especially Chapter IV, "Control Starts with Planning." (See also Chapter 20 in *this* book.)

TARGET DATES Set target dates for completion of every project. If your boss sets deadlines for you, suggest to him/her that you set them together. If this seems impossible, check the references in "Priorities" above.

CONTROL Plan ahead for possible crises and deadlines, and anticipate your own action. The secret is taking control of your life.

QUICK RELAXING Take time out from your schedule (if only for five minutes) every day and relax. Detach yourself from the job and use pleasant scenes or thoughts to revitalize yourself. Another technique you might want to try: Become aware when your breathing is

WORK STRESS BUFFERS

shallow and fast. When this does happen, briefly stop what you are doing and analyze what you are doing externally or internally. Take control and breathe more slowly and more deeply. This will help reduce those feelings of anxiety. (See also Chapter 17.)

MORE QUICK RELAXING Instead of taking six seconds and popping a valium, try using the same six seconds and relax for free. It is a simple three-step process, each step taking just two seconds. Step one: Stop what you're doing and take a long, slow, deep breath. Step two: Smile sincerely as you are inhaling. Step three: Slowly exhale, letting your shoulders relax while mentally repeating to yourself, "I'm relaxing."

MORE QUICK RELAXING Another six second freebie. You may like it and try it for more than six seconds. Step one: place your elbows on a table. Step two: lightly touch your first three fingertips to your forehead above each eyebrow. Step three: hold this position for at least four seconds, while monitoring your breathing. In seconds you will, amazingly, feel waves of relaxation flowing through your body.

MENTAL TIME OUTS Make a conscious effort to relax yourself prior to a presentation, meeting, or important phone call.

WALK Take a walk (even for only five minutes) to keep your body refreshed and alert. Make it pleasant and greet people you meet along the way.

NOISE Check out the noise level of your work area. Be creative in finding ways of reducing it. Noise is a big contributor to stress.

INTERRUPTABLE TIME Schedule specific times that you *will permit interruptions.*

Return all phone calls 1/2 hour before lunch and 1/2 hour before closing. People generally are not interested in carrying on long discourses at these times of day.

OVERTIME   Do not spend eight straight hours in your office or workplace if you can avoid it. No eating over your desk or staying that extra 1/2 hour after quitting time, either!

MEETINGS   Begin meetings at unusual times (9:47, 2:09) for variety. Announce when the meeting will end and stick to that schedule.

MORE ON MEETINGS   If the meeting is to be very short, keep everybody standing.

TELEPHONE   Begin telephone conversations with the reason you called. Not "How are you?" or "What's new?"

COPE NOW   Deal with stressful problems immediately. It is better to deal with short-term stress instead of letting it become long-term anxiety and discomfort.

WORRY LIST[*]   Take control of your problems and worries. Periodically make a worry list: write down the problems that concern you and beside each one write down what you are going to do. It is easier to deal with problems once they are in the open.

ASSERTIVENESS   Say what you feel. Be open, honest, direct, but don't consciously hurt the other person. You violate your own rights (and hurt yourself) if you act non-assertively. You violate others' rights (and hurt them) if you are aggressive. Learning the differences among the three types of behavior and how to incorporate

---

[*]From Karl Albrecht, *Stress and the Manager.* Adapted with permission of Prentice-Hall, Inc.

more assertive behaviors into your life is possible through assertiveness training. The result can produce less stress not only on the job but throughout your life. More in Chapter 20.

CAREER CHANGES Stress may be so overwhelming for you that a change in your work environment may be the only solution. This could be either a change in the present job (by revising job descriptions or shifting positions), or a completely new job with a new organization. Even if a job change is not in your immediate future, it may not be far away. Most American workers will change careers several times during their work life. An excellent book is available that can help you be as prepared as possible: *What Color is Your Parachute?* The very practical book (make sure it's the current edition—it is now being updated annually) includes a fascinating workbook ("The Quick Job-Hunting Map").

EVENINGS At the end of the working day, before you go home, write down the five most important things you have to do tomorrow. After doing this, number them in the order of their importance. At the beginning of the next day, start working on the most important thing. Do not be concerned if you do not finish all five things because you will always be working on the most important thing!

Your evenings are a precious commodity. Be assertive with yourself and your job if you find yourself taking home work on a regular basis. Avoid any kind of activity that is even related to the job; create a pleasurable diversity.

WORK POLLUTION Check out the following areas of your work environment: visual attractiveness, light level, people around you. If any of these are creating pressure, creatively consider ways of changing the situation. Rearrange a desk, hang a picture, paint a wall, bring in a plant. Be resourceful. Even small changes will help. If changes are not possible, don't give up. Offset the negative condition by engaging in some type of compensatory activity during breaks, lunch periods, after work (exercise, sports, walks, hobbies, meditation).

FUN BREAKS AT WORK Even during the work day you can be in control and make the time more pleasurable. Create short periods of diversion (5 minutes, 15 minutes, 30 minutes, whatever). Here are some ideas: reading a favorite magazine or novel, listening to cassette tapes with music or motivational ideas, breathing/relaxing exercises, walking or meeting someone new at work during a break, wearing clothes that make you feel good, changing what you eat for lunch and where.

JOB CHANGES When you have a new job or a change in the responsibilities of an old job, take advantage of the situation. Use the opportunity to organize yourself, ask for help, delegate whenever possible, verbalize your expectations, needs, limitations to yourself, colleagues and superiors. Above all, accept your mistakes as learning opportunities, and always be patient with yourself.

SUPERIORS AND STRESS Share your ideas, hopes, and plans for stress reduction with your colleagues, but especially your superiors. Encourage them to make stress awareness and reduction an organizational concern and priority. The statistics prove that less-stressed employees are more productive! Even minimal amounts of time off during the work day for stress reducing activities pay big dividends.

SIT DOWN AND RELAX FOR 3 MINUTES! What to do at work when you are becoming overwhelmed by the pressures? Here is a brief exercise which will help clear your mind and revive a body that is tensing up. These techniques are not substitutes for a regular physical activity program, or for the more in-depth relaxation procedures described in Chapter 17. Nevertheless, this 3-minute routine will help a lot when there is not time for anything more!

Begin these exercises sitting *straight* and toward the edge of a chair. *Smile* while you are enjoying the good feelings they produce!

1. *Breathe:* Take 4-5 slow, deep breaths and clear your mind of all concerns and thoughts.

2. *Neck & shoulders:* Raise your shoulders, trying to touch your ears with them. At the same time stretch out your arms in front of you. Tense your arms and shoulders and hold for 5 seconds. Then release....
Raise your shoulders again. This time stretch out your arms to the sides. Tense your arms and shoulders and hold for 5 seconds. Then release....Roll your head gently twice to the right and then twice to the left.

3. *Back:* Raise your arms above your head and pretend you are using your hands and arms to climb a ladder. Slowly and rhythmically continue for 10 seconds. Then release....
While facing forward in your chair, *slowly* and *gently* turn your torso to the right as far as you can, trying if you can to grasp the back of the chair. Then turn to the left. Repeat this step again.

4. *Legs:* Lift your right leg. Roll your foot in a circle 5 times. Repeat for the left leg. Repeat the complete step again....
Lift both legs. Bend your feet toward your head. Hold for 5 seconds. Then bend your feet away from your head. Hold for 5 seconds. Then release.

5. *Breathe:* Pick a pleasant and peaceful place to go to in your mind. Close your eyes. Release any tension you might feel anywhere in your body. For the next minute or so just breathe slowly and deeply.

6. *Reality:* Return to your activities refreshed and relieved. Use this three-minute mind and body break at the slightest hint of creeping tension.

Work Bibliography

Bolles, Richard N., *The Three Boxes of Life and How to Get Out of Them*
Bolles, Richard N., *What Color is Your Parachute?*
Fanning, Tony and Robbie, *Get It All Done and Still Be Human*
Freudenberger, Herbert, *Burn Out: How to Beat the High Cost of Success*
Hall, Francine and Douglas, *The Two-Career Couple*
Jackson, Tom, *Guerrilla Tactics in the Job Market*
Lakein, Alan, *How to Get Control of Your Time and Your Life*
Mackenzie, R. Alec, *The Time Trap*
Phelps, Stanlee and Austin, Nancy, *The Assertive Woman*
Terkel, Studs, *Working*
Walker, C. Eugene, *Learn to Relax: 13 Ways to Reduce Tension*
Welch, I. David, Medeiros, Donald, and Tate, George, *Beyond Burnout*

The Born Loser

14

Leisure Stress Buffers

Stress-Buffers SUGGESTIONS NOTES IDEAS TIPS RESOURCES SHARING POTPOURRI

"If you would not age, you must make everything you do touched with play, play of the body, play of the thought, of emotions. If you do, you will belong to that special class of people who find joy and happiness in every act, in every moment. Those to whom leisure is the one thing valuable."

Dr. George Sheehan
Running and Being, the Total Experience

"You must first be convinced that LEISURE is important, that you want more of it and are willing to change anything in life to get it."

Haney and Boenisch

MINUTE VACATIONS Start small. Teach yourself *again* how to take 30 to 60 seconds to enjoy the small, fleeting beauties of life. When did you last pause long enough to really enjoy any of these...

- smell of a flower
- sight of clear, cool water
- a walk through leaves in the autumn
- a sunrise or sunset
- smell of burning wood
- a walk by a creek
- feel of leather
- feel of warm, moist lips
- a piece of art

- smell of something baking
- warmth of the sun
- a cool breeze
- silence of the woods
- a rainbow
- freshly fallen snow
- autumn leaves
- taste of popcorn
- birds singing

Take a few minutes and add here any other experiences that make you feel more alive:

Many such experiences briefly enter each day. Look for them today, and take a minute vacation with them.

SMALL ESCAPES Do you know what makes you happy? What relaxes you? Give yourself permission to escape mentally for brief moments into an unstructured world where you can relax and have fun. Some possibilities:

Mentally travel to:

- a deserted beach
- a log cabin
- a tree house
- the woods

- grandma's house
- a vacation spot of your dreams
- a warm, flowery meadow

Try:

- a warm bath
- cocktails, candlelight and incense in the bathroom
- a picnic on the living-room floor with music
- a sauna
- reading a good book in bed
- sitting in front of a crackling fire with the lights out
- listening to a favorite album with earphones
- a slow shampoo from a loved one
- people watching
- window-shopping
- spending an entire evening surrounded only by candlelight.
- bus riding for pleasure
- doing crossword or jigsaw puzzles
- bookstore browsing
- visiting craft shows and flea markets
- raising pets
- letter writing
- flying model airplanes or kites
- quilting
- wine-making
- flower-arranging
- watching educational TV

TELEVISION   Make this invention a real source of relaxing entertainment and leisure. Preview the weekly schedule and decide in advance on several programs that you would enjoy alone or as a family or with friends. Turn on the television immediately before the scheduled program, and turn it off when the show is over. Stay away from violent or anxiety-producing topics. (You know what relaxes you or makes you uptight.) If the local or national news becomes depressing or overwhelming—turn it off. Try a weekly news magazine as a source of current events. Pick and choose what you read, watch, and hear!

FRIENDS   Rekindle friendships. Send out invitations several weeks in advance for a potluck supper. Announce in your invitation the starting and ending time if this will keep it from becoming a hassle. Try potlucks with food themes. Try them in the neighborhood as a way of making new friends.

REWARDS Tie your leisure to projects. Do a chore or task and have a specific leisure reward planned for yourself when you finish. Never deny yourself the reward. This works especially well with children. Try eating out once a week as a reward if everyone pitches in and cleans the house right after work, or Saturday, or *anytime*!

SPACE Create a specific area in the home for projects and hobbies. Even a section of a room is enough. Make it a quiet, relaxing place anyone in the home can use whenever he/she wants to think, unwind, create, or just be.

MISCELLANEOUS Take a non-credit class or read books to relax or learn a new hobby. Trade skills with someone so you can learn from each other the new talent or hobby. Buy season tickets for something you enjoy (you are then *committed* to attend). Take 20 minutes at the beginning of every month and actually schedule on a calendar something leisurely to do *every* week (as a minimum).

BIOFEEDBACK Stress causes changes to occur continuously within your body, producing variations in your peripheral skin temperature, sweat gland activity, brain wave activity, heart rate, blood pressure and muscle contractions, to name a few. While these fluctuations are normally imperceptible, biofeedback instruments can amplify them, usually electronically, providing immediate information on the body-mind interaction. Biofeedback training is a way of quickly learning to control a wide variety of body functions that were once thought to be beyond conscious control. Relaxation, autogenic exercises and visualization are key ingredients used in conjunction with the actual biofeedback training. The benefit in learning to control any or all of these body functions is that you can *prevent* the occurrence or severity of many of the annoying results of stress: cold, clammy hands, tense neck, pounding heart, and others.

LEISURE STRESS BUFFERS

DOTS?....WHAT'S WITH THE DOTS? Buy yourself a package of adhesive dots (any color that is pleasing and restful to you). Most office supply stores carry them. Place them in strategic locations in your environment. Some suggestions include the telephone, file cabinet, desk drawer, mirrors or dashboard of the car. The dots can serve as gentle reminders to practice breathing, relaxation, desk exercises, positive thinking or any other eustress skill.

LUNCH TIME "HIDEAWAYS" How do you spend your lunch time? Do you eat at the same place with the same people daily? Maybe you're cheating yourself. Those 30 or 60 minutes in the middle of your eight-hour day could be the most rewarding. This time offers you the opportunity for relaxation, fun and self-discovery. Try some of the following suggestions.

- *Health clubs.* How about engaging in a physical fitness program during lunch? Talk to the people around you who are working out at lunch time and compare their complaints about tension, fatigue and headaches with the non-exercisers.
- *Museums.* Try concentrating on one section at a time. Some of the larger museums even have cafeterias—you would not even have to miss lunch!
- *Television.* Perhaps a lounge chair, feet up and your favorite soap opera could be another way of getting away from the tension at work. If going home is out of the question, bring a small black and white portable TV to work and share with those co-workers who enjoy the same shows.
- *Beauty break.* Treat your body to some luxury and get a haircut, shampoo, massage, sauna or facial session. Men as well as women are trying this one more and more.
- *Golf course.* Nine holes is probably out of the question, but what about taking your frustrations out on a bucket of golf balls? You do not even have to know how to play golf to do this.

- *Flower shop, nursery.* If you like plants, spend your time becoming more familiar with shrubs, trees and flowers. Being among plants away from the job is extremely restful.
- *Cemetery.* To some a trip through the cemetery sounds morbid, but if you are interested in local history or researching genealogy, it can be fascinating.
- *Home decorating.* Take as many lunch hours as necessary and browse through shops that carry paint, furniture and wallpaper. It takes time to get the rooms of your home or apartment the way you want, and it's easier when you are not under pressure to make immediate decisions. If you work 50 weeks a year, that gives you up to 250 lunch hours!
- *Class.* Start a lunch time exercise class with other co-workers. Or find out some of their hobby areas and learn from one another.
- *Greeting card shop.* Do you always dash in the last minute to buy that greeting card? It is much more pleasant to shop ahead of time and find you have a much larger selection. Put it on your calendar to buy cards once a month.
- *Public library.* Try visiting the periodical section or the music section. Listening to a soothing selection with earphones while browsing through a favorite magazine is great for the mind and body.
- *Shopping or browsing* in beautiful places such as art galleries, fine jewelry shops, antique stores or expensive boutiques has a very tranquil effect on many people. Stores of these types are very accustomed to having people ''Just looking'' and it costs nothing.
- *More...* Lunch on a park bench, visit a travel agency or hobby store, take a walking tour of the city. Think up others. Try them. Consider them daily rewards.

LEISURE MAGAZINES Subscribe to a leisure magazine. It could be any one of dozens that deal with a favorite pastime, hobby, craft, special interest, or activity that you currently enjoy or would like to try. For a few dollars a month or even less, the magazine will provide a few regular hours of fun. Any library can help you explore the wide range of magazines currently available.

PERSONAL PREFERENCES Sometimes people find it difficult to enjoy leisure activities because they don't know what they like (or have perhaps forgotten). Take a few leisurely minutes now and list your preferences. Do you like to play alone, with your age group, with both sexes? Do you like physical, intellectual, social, emotional or creative activities? What kind of feelings would you like from your leisure (achievement, recognition, relaxation, pleasure)? Do you want to spend your leisure time in town, in the country, by a lake, in a forest, on a beach? When do you like to be leisurely (morning, evening, on weekends, during holidays)? Pick the sports, games, activities, hobbies, crafts, or pastimes that match your preferences.

SCHEDULED LEISURE Until you learn to be a leisurely person, on a regular basis, without feeling guilty— carefully schedule times to enjoy leisure. Think about leisure as you would think about a business trip, a doctor's appointment, a meal or any other scheduled commitment you would not miss.

Leisure for many people is enjoying friends. So many times, when we see or talk to special people, we tend to end our conversation with "Let's get together sometime." You know what usually happens: you never get together. Be assertive with yourself and those good friends. Take the extra few minutes to actually *arrange* something specific. People who do so rarely regret it.

Perhaps you are one of those many who procrastinate or feel guilty about leisure; *scheduled* leisure is a good way to begin. Consider classes and workshops in sports, games, wine-tasting, cooking, backpacking, dog obedience, fly tying, poetry appreciation, horseshoes, card games.... Local park and recreation offices and community colleges (ask for the "community services" program) usually provide exciting possibilities for very little expense.

SHARING WORK AND LEISURE   Individuals and families sometimes complain about not having any time to relax because of "all the chores around the house." One family solved this problem by selecting a specific evening and time when they *all* shared the chores. They blocked out every Wednesday from 5:30 to 7:00. Every family member (mom, dad and the two children) had mutually agreeable duties which resulted in the most important chores getting done and ensured the work load was equalized. Tasks were rotated as much as possible. Everyone worked hard and afterwards all were rewarded with supper at a restaurant. The immediate reward is very important. Their weekends, previously filled with work, are now scheduled for leisure activities.

LEISURE RENEWAL   Leisure is not just sitting and relaxing, although sometimes it includes this activity. Leisure is discovering the playful child in you and giving it permission to laugh and frolic again. Leisure is anything that will *renew* your mind, body, and spirit!

Leisure Bibliography

Ahl, David H. (Ed.), *Basic Computer Games*
Bammel, G. and Burrus-Bammel, Lei Lane, *Leisure and Human Behavior*
Benson, Herbert and Klipper, Miriam, *The Relaxation Response*
Bolles, Richard N., *The Three Boxes of Life and How to Get Out of Them*
Buxbaum, Robert and Micheli, Lyle, *Sports for Life: Fitness Training, Injury Prevention and Nutrition*
Downing, George, *The Massage Book*
Fast, Julius, *The Pleasure Book*
Fluegelman, A., *The New Games Book*
Greenberg, Robyn, Harmon, Rick and Henshaw, Jean (Eds.), *The Leisure Alternatives Catalog: Food for Mind and Body*

Gregg, Elizabeth and Boston Children's Medical Center Staff, *What to Do When There's Nothing to Do*

Grunfeld, Frederick V. (Ed.), *Games of the World: How to Make Them, How to Play Them, How They Came to Be*

Hendricks, Gay and Wills, Russel, *The Centering Book: Awareness Activities for Children, Parents and Teachers*

Johnson, June, *838 Ways to Amuse a Child*

Kostrubala, Thaddeus, *Joy of Running*

LeShan, Lawrence, *How to Meditate*

Ryan, Regina S. and Travis, John W., *Wellness Workbook*

Stein, Lincoln D., *Family Games*

U.S. Government Printing Office, *An Introduction to Running: One Step at a Time*

Walker, C. Eugene, *Learn to Relax*

Weinstein, Matt and Goodman, Joel, *Playfair: Everybody's Guide to Non-Competitive Play*

The Born Loser

15

Mind Stress Buffers

Stress-Buffers SUGGESTIONS NOTES IDEAS TIPS RESOURCES SHARING POTPOURRI

MEDITATION — Giving your mind a rest period is important. Meditation comes in many forms. Some, like Transcendental Meditation (TM), involve money and classes to learn. Other forms can be very simple, yet just as effective depending on how serious you are. A good book to begin with is *How to Meditate* by Lawrence LeShan.

RELAXATION — Almost every self-help or stress book mentions this very important way of revitalizing your physical and intellectual energies. Some provide extensive written instructions for systematically relaxing (see Chapter 17). Advertisements for cassette tapes appear in more and more popular magazines. Almost anyone with a calm, soothing voice, however, could record instructions onto tape for personal use. This technique can be used almost anywhere, in any amount of time available from 30 seconds to 30 minutes. This simple remedy is free and can be one of the most effective means of combatting stress if it is used consistently and conscientiously.

TELEVISION — Sell the TV if it is interfering with your life! At least move the set to an out-of-the-way room of the house. Let TV be a source of intellectual stimulation, not a millstone that pulls you down into mindless oblivion. See also Chapter 14 for more ideas.

READING
- Visit your local college and/or public library.
- Set a goal to read one book a week, or one a month, or some comfortable number; then *do* it!
- Make time to read. The time can be short (10 minutes) or long periods. Let reading become a habit.
- Ask your friends for recommendations of good books that are in line with your tastes.
- Don't forget magazines. But be selective; don't have 8 to 10 magazines arriving every week unless you can realistically read them. Make reading relaxing, not a chore.
- Read for personal growth. For example, read Gail Sheehy's bestselling book, *Passages: Predictable Crises of Adult Life.* Locate the developmental stage at which you now find yourself and the predictable crises at this stage. With an understanding of these crises, you can become more empowered to reach potential and gain more positive control of your life.

THOUGHT CHANGING   You are in control of what you think. If you find yourself being plagued by negative, stressful, depressing thoughts, stop for 5 to 10 seconds and mentally tell the unwanted thoughts to "STOP." Then, immediately start creating positive images of relaxation, tranquility, and pleasant relationships with others.

TRAVEL
- Draw a 100 mile radius around your home and plan one-day trips to places you have never been.
- Find out about the lower travel costs offered by travel groups and on airlines offering "super-savers."
- Change your own perspective on what is or can be relaxing! You don't have to go to Las Vegas to enjoy the sun.
- Try camping instead of "motelling" it.

DISCUSSION GROUPS   Organize a discussion group of friends to meet periodically and discuss current issues, books, travel, hobbies, plays, music, local history, recreation, politics, religion, even ways to deal with stress!

YOGA
- Learn to relax utilizing this Far Eastern method of cultivating good health. It can give you a new vital source of energy, help in quieting the mind, and a new way to handle stress.
- Enroll in a course through a local college or YWCA/YMCA group.
- Good reading material: *Yoga for Women*, *Yoga for Beauty*

OUT OF CONTROL? Many people continually accept more and more positions, tasks, or jobs. Overload results: feelings of being overwhelmed, pressured, unable to do justice to anything. There are no superwomen or supermen. It is not a sign of weakness to accept the fact that you have limited time and energy. If you're overwhelmed now, carefully evaluate each obligation and make some choices about what has to go. Be careful about taking on new responsibilities without carefully evaluating the ramifications.

DISSATISFIED WITH YOURSELF? As hard as it may be to accept, you allowed yourself to be who you are now. And you can change yourself. Try to identify *specifically,* in writing, what you would like to change. Decide how you can use more of the strengths you already have or develop different ones. Look around at friends or acquaintances who have strengths you would like. Ask them how they developed them.

GET ORGANIZED Get more done in less time. Organization is a matter of habit. Analyze what is wasting your time and why. Begin by prioritizing things, organizing your work environment, preventing interruptions, and delegating responsibilities. See Chapter 20 for some ideas in this area.

NEW AVENUES Explore some new sources of intellectual development. Enroll in a college course covering a special subject you've been wanting to know about. Forget the stress of exams by signing up for "audit" (enrolling for informational purposes only, not for credit). Try a new hobby. Invite a friend to join you in developing new insights and interests. Be creative and adventurous.

PEAKS Analyze those times you have considered "peak experiences" (those times which have made you feel "high" on life itself) and figure out just why they were peaks. Then plan for them to happen by including the same people, events or places in your life at regular intervals. One place to start is the checklist in the Leisure chapter, "Minute Vacations and Small Escapes."

SPIRITUAL GROWTH For many the answer to satisfaction, being loved, feeling important, and finding meaning in life is found in a special, close relationship with God—a Supreme Being, higher consciousness, Buddha, universal life force, or other personal concept of a spirit which transcends human experience. Some find their way to God through books. A few which have helped others in "opening the door" are listed at the end of this chapter.

Others find their personal God through meditation or contemplation. Books that will assist you in this refreshing and insightful process include: *How to Meditate* and *The Inner Source.* Personal prayer goes well with meditation (before, during or after) and can be a powerful source of insight and comfort.

Some people experience their God when they become a part of a community. Different religious groups have their own unique approaches and atmospheres. Many people find the most supportive and compatible group by actually visiting them for a service or two.

Another way of meeting your God is through friends. Ask them about their faith and beliefs. Find out how they came to experience the joys of a loving God. Most people won't push their beliefs or religion and are very sincere about sharing when asked.

Mind Bibliography

Benson, Herbert M.O., *The Relaxation Response*
The Bible
de Chardin, Teilhard, *Building the Earth*
Emmons, Michael, *The Inner Source: A Guide to Meditative Therapy*
Fanning, Tony and Robbie, *Get It All Done and Still Be Human*
Gibran, Kahlil, *The Prophet*
Goldberg, Phillip and Kaufman, Daniel, *Natural Sleep: How to Get Your Share*
Hutschnecker, Arnold, *The Will to Live*
Lakein, Alan, *How to Get Control of Your Time and Your Life*
LeShan, Lawrence, *How to Meditate: A Guide to Self-Discovery*
LeShan, Lawrence, *You Can Fight for Your Life: Emotional Factors in the Treatment of Cancer*
Mackenzie, Alec, *The Time Trap*
Mandino, Og, *The Greatest Miracle in the World*
Moody, Raymond, *Life After Life*
Peale, Norman Vincent, *The Power of Positive Thinking*
Phelan, Nancy and Volin, Michael, *Yoga for Women*
Sheehy, Gail, *Passages: Predictable Crises of Adult Life*
Simonton, O. Carl, Matthews-Simonton, Stephanie and Creighton, James L., *Getting Well Again*
Volin, Michael and Phelan, Nancy, *Yoga for Beauty*
Walker, C. Eugene, *Learn to Relax*

16
Body Stress Buffers

Stress-Buffers SUGGESTIONS NOTES IDEAS TIPS RESOURCES SHARING POTPOURRI

"Undoubtedly, the waste of a mind is a terrible thing. The waste of a soul is worse. But it all begins with the waste of the body."

Dr. George Sheehan
Running and Being, the Total Experience

SUPPORT GROUPS   Almost every community offers support groups through county extension offices, colleges, school districts, YMCA's, YWCA's, mental health centers, or private organizations. Such groups are often free and exist for exercising, nutrition, dieting, smoking, relaxation. Dealing with any of these areas is much easier if it is done with others.

EXERCISE   The first step in doing something for your body is to *decide* to do it. Do not increase your exercise or start a program without making sure you are in reasonably good health. If you are over 35 or have any history of physical problems, have a medical examination and a physician's approval and advice on a good exercise program. It would help to choose a doctor who is physically fit and a regular exerciser! Give exercise a high priority in your life. Take your time, develop good habits, and most important of all, make exercise a pleasant growth experience. A wealth of books is available. Browse through any library or bookstore for titles listed at the end of this chapter. More on exercise in Chapter 18.

NUTRITION AND DIET   Read up on nutrition and dieting. Some communities have classes or even nutrition counseling available. Study your eating habits and decide what you need to change, if anything, to create the best balance. If you need to lose a small or large amount of weight, do not go on a crash diet. Adopt a long-term program of readjusting your eating habits to keep the joy in eating while taking in fewer calories. If you are extremely overweight, have a medical examination and get your doctor's advice. Books on this subject are many and varied. We've listed a few later in the chapter. Also, Chapter 17 expands on this topic.

SMOKING   *Give it up, completely!* Do anything: read, visit professionals, talk to people—anything that will move you to break the habit. Physical exercise will many times help greatly in stopping. Talk to the American Cancer Society or the Lung Association—they have free literature.

DRINKING   You may feel you should change your alcohol habits. Start slowly. Find other sources of relaxation: exercise, sports, friends who will be supportive, reading, relaxation exercises, meditation, music, anything that will be right for you. Cut back with the help of local organizations (their services are usually free).

DRUGS   We refer not to the "hard" drugs so much as to those everyday recreational drugs that have made their way into your life—tranquilizers, caffeine, nicotine, or any medicine to which you can develop a habit. Coffee, tea and soft drinks all contain habit-forming caffeine. Taper off gradually. You do not have to give up caffeine completely, but reduce your intake to a level that will not add to your stress reaction.

QUIET PLACE   If you do not have a special place in your home that can be a quiet, personal, and private retreat—be good to yourself and create one *today*! If you live with others, let them know about your quiet place so they can respect your privacy and needs when you are there. Invite them to use your retreat or to create their own. Children can benefit from this just as much as adults. Help them early in life to find the value and strength in being in a personal, restful place all their own. If physical space is not available, you can develop a "quiet corner" and encourage others to respect your needs.

SEX Sometimes sex therapy is needed to resolve some difficulties. Usually, a trusting, honest attitude and good communication go a long way. Some books can be excellent guides to deeper fulfillment and adventure: *Joy of Sex, The Massage Book, Love Without Fear, Our Bodies, Ourselves.*

HOLISTIC HEALTH Throughout this book we have emphasized the importance of concern for mind, body, spirit and relationships. Some excellent books are available to help you understand and appreciate the fulfillment that can result from the integration of your mind, spirit, and body into a holistic unity. *High Level Wellness* is one of the best. It contains an extensive annotated bibliography for further reading.

TECHNIQUES FOR HEALTHFUL LIVING [*] People are healthy when they believe life gets better with each passing year. The following suggestions can be practiced by anyone and will definitely add to your well-being.

1. Change old patterns by trying new and different ways of doing things. Break taboos and drink *white* wine with red meat, go to an X-rated movie, buy the bikini you have always wanted (and wear it!).

---

[*]Developed by Arthur Ulene, M.D., and reproduced by permission of the author.

2. Be assertive and learn to say ''no''! This simple word will give you freedom and control of your life. Practice by saying ''no'' aloud.

3. Don't hide your ''Sunday's best'' or your keepsakes. *Use* that sterling silver and silk. They don't do much for you put away in a closet.

4. Take time to look at the rainbows and smell the flowers. Find a place and stare at the sky. If you must, shut the door and take the phone off the hook. Do it daily.

5. Listen to your feelings and respect them. Trust the connection between body and mind.

BODY IMAGE — Stand in front of a full-length mirror and closely analyze your style of dress, posture, hairstyle, facial expressions, weight. Dissatisfied with the way you think you look? Maybe a major overhaul is out of the question, but consider small, inexpensive ways of changing what you do not like.

The Born Loser

Body Bibliography

Abrahamson, E.M. and Pezet, A.W., *Body, Mind, and Sugar*
Ardell, Donald, *High Level Wellness: An Alternative to Doctors, Drugs and Disease*
Boston Women's Health Collective, *Our Bodies, Ourselves: A Book By and For Women*
Brody, Jane, *Jane Brody's Nutrition Book*
Brown, Barbara B., *Stress and the Art of Biofeedback*
Buxbaum, Robert, *Sports for Life*
Campbell, Greg, *The Joy of Jumping*
Chesser, Eustace, *Love Without Fear*
Comfort, Alex, *Joy of Sex*
Downing, George, *The Massage Book*
Ewald, Ellen B., *Recipes for a Small Planet*
Fonda, Jane, *Jane Fonda's Workout Book*
Fredericks, Carlton, *Look Younger, Feel Healthier*
Getchell, Bud and Anderson, Wayne, *Being Fit: A Personal Guide*
Haimes, Leonard and Tyson, Richard, *How to Triple Your Energy*
Hastings, Arthur, Fadiman, James and Gordon, James, *Health for the Whole Person: The Complete Guide to Holistic Medicine*
Jacobson, Howard, *Racewalk to Fitness*
Kostrubala, Thaddeus, *Joy of Running*
Kuntzleman, Charles T., *Diet Free*
Lappe, Frances Moore, *Diet for a Small Planet*
Martin, Elizabeth, *The Over-30; 6-Week All Natural Health and Beauty Plan*
Martinez, Pam, *Sugarless Cooking*
Millman, Dan, *Whole Body Fitness: Training Mind, Body and Spirit*
Nyad, Diana and Hogan, Candice Lyle, *Diana Nyad's Basic Training for Women*
Orbach, Susie, *Fat Is a Feminist Issue*
Rodale Press, Inc., *Executive Fitness Newsletter*
U.S. Government Printing Office, *An Introduction to Running: One Step at a Time* (S/N 017-001-00425-1)
Vaughn, William, *Low Salt Secrets for Your Diet*

17
Stress Relief: Relaxation

Try a simple test. Place one hand on your chest and the other hand on your stomach. Breathe normally for 30 seconds. If the hand on your chest is moving, you are like most people who are not using the simplest yet most effective stress management technique available.

Breathing affects your whole body. When you are angry your breathing probably becomes irregular. Fear or stress usually produces quick and shallow breaths. A relaxed state is characterized by breathing that is slow, deep and regular. When you take a few seconds to breathe slowly, deeply and regularly in a stressful situation, you produce a state of relaxation.

Correct breathing actually short-circuits the stress response and promotes relaxation. In addition, correct breathing can strengthen and condition the pulmonary system, building up a respiratory reserve and increasing the capacity of the blood to carry oxygen throughout the body. The whole cardiovascular system can be enhanced, and nerves calmed, by using breathing techniques.

The key to correct breathing is to allow your diaphragm to do what it was designed to do. This simple muscle, located beneath your ribs, is supposed to expand *downward* when you inhale. This means your stomach should move out gently. In normal breathing, your rib cage can move outward—but not a lot. Most people try to keep their stomachs pulled in and breathe by raising their rib cages each time they inhale. This is awkward and takes a lot of energy, continually lifting a heavy rib cage when it was not designed to move so much in normal breathing. Exhaling should be a very gentle, effortless process: your diaphragm is relaxed and it pushes the air out as your stomach comes in.

Try the test again. This time as you hold your hand on your stomach, try lifting your hand by gently pushing out your stomach. You will be inhaling effortlessly as you do this. Breathe slowly for several minutes to become accustomed to the feeling.

In *any* stressful situation, no matter where you are, you can consciously use a simple breathing technique to reduce the tension and produce some relaxation. This technique, which takes only 35 to 40 seconds, consists of the following steps:
1. Stand or sit as erect as possible and try to take your mind off of the stressful situation or activities around you.
2. Take a slow, deep breath while counting to three.
3. Hold your breath gently for a count of three.
4. Exhale slowly for a count of three.
5. Pause for a count of three.
6. Repeat this sequence three times.
7. Return to your activities.

How Do You Spell "Relaxation"?

Recently, when asked how they relaxed, people responded in a variety of ways:

"Let me watch a good football game and I'll relax."

"I take an aspirin and go to bed."

"For me, it's a scotch-on-the-rocks while watching the evening news."

"A favorite rock album through headphones while studying is relaxation for me."

"When I need to relax, I run a hot bath and soak for five minutes."

Unfortunately, not one of these individuals is relaxing well enough to significantly reduce tension and stress! At best, they are engaged in a favorite pastime that might be fun and satisfying.

The relaxation response is a physical and mental technique that counteracts the stress response, creating a return to normal. Balance is achieved within the system. Complete relaxation involves learning to recognize and feel tension in every muscle of the body, and how to release it.

Four basic elements are required to learn the relaxation response:

1. *A quiet place to practice.* Pick a time and a place where you are unlikely to be interrupted for 20 to 30 minutes. It helps to use the same location, at the same time, and to tell the children, spouse, friends what you will be doing. This special place should be as quiet and comfortable as possible. Dim the lights and loosen any tight clothing before practicing. You should also avoid practicing immediately before retiring (you will probably fall asleep and won't learn the techniques) or after a meal (your body is too busy with digestion to concentrate on muscle relaxation).

2. *A comfortable position.* Use a favorite chair or sofa which supports your body evenly. Avoid lying down on the floor or a bed, or taking another position in which you are likely to fall asleep. Your head should be supported, however, so you can relax your neck.

A phrase or word to help you concentrate may be helpful as you learn the technique of relaxing. Some suggestions include:

PHRASES	WORDS
I am relaxing	Relax
I feel peaceful	Peace
My mind is quiet	Quiet
I am calm	Calm
I feel healing and energy	Healing
I am being renewed	Renew

After you have mastered the skill of relaxing, your word or phrase will be your key to activating the relaxation response. Anytime, anywhere, you can mentally say this word or phrase and your mind will work with your body to produce a relaxed state in five to ten minutes. That's your goal.

4. *A passive attitude* is the last element needed to learn the relaxation response. Follow the "relaxation instructions" and *allow* the relaxation to develop. Allow the tension to flow out of your body, effortlessly. Do not try to force yourself or work too hard. Just let it happen.

Deep Muscle Relaxation

Deep relaxation is one of the most effective yet simplest techniques you can employ to reduce the effects of stress. It is also free and can be learned on your own in less than two weeks, practicing 15 to 30 minutes a day.

The instructions provided on the next pages can be memorized, tape recorded by you or someone with a soothing voice, or read aloud by a friend. (See also the commercial aids listed at the end of this chapter.)

After the instructions are completed, remain in this relaxed state for as long as you wish. If any tension creeps in, simply let it go as soon as you notice it. When you want to continue with your other activities, slowly open your eyes and continue to sit quietly for 15 to 30 seconds. Then slowly move and resume activity. You should feel refreshed, awake and calm.

After using the instructions or tape five to seven times, try relaxing without them. You will find that you can *mentally* progress through the process in less and less time. You should also be able to begin relaxing completely, without going through the tensing stage, by simply focusing on a muscle group and allowing it to relax. At the same time, allow the relaxation in one area to flow into another area. Eventually you should be able to use your relaxation skills at any time and place, without interrupting your activities, by simply repeating your relaxation word or phrase several times when you notice muscle tension. Once activated, your relaxation response will take over and produce a relaxed state for you in just a few minutes.

RELAXATION TECHNIQUE: Mental Relaxation Place
(Five to ten minutes) *
1. Select a comfortable sitting or reclining position.
2. Close your eyes, and think about a place that you have been before that represents your ideal place for physical and mental relaxation. (It should be a quiet environment, perhaps the seashore, the mountains, or even your own back yard. If you can't think of an ideal relaxation place, then create one in your mind.)
3. Now imagine that you are actually in your ideal relaxation place. Imaging that you are seeing all the colors, hearing the sounds, smelling the aromas. Just lie back, and enjoy your soothing, rejuvenating environment.
4. Feel the peacefulness, the calmness, and imagine your whole body and mind being renewed and refreshed.
5. After five to ten minutes, slowly open your eyes and stretch. You have the realization that you may instantly return to your relaxation place whenever you desire, and experience a peacefulness and calmness in body and mind.

RELAXATION TECHNIQUE: Thinking About Body Parts
(Twenty minutes) *
1. Select a comfortable place to lie down. Remove shoes, loosen belt or light clothing. Stretch out on your back, arms resting by your sides, feet slightly apart, eyes gently closed.
2. Think to yourself, "I am now going to relax completely. When I awaken I will feel fully refreshed."

---

*Developed by Dr. Cary Howard McCarthy. From *Stress and the Art of Biofeedback* by Barbara B. Brown. © 1977 by Barbara B. Brown. Used by permission of Bantam Books, Inc. All rights reserved.

3. Think about your feet, wiggle your toes, flex your ankles. Then "let go"—let go of all the tension, and let your feet rest limp and heavy.
4. Think of the lower part of your legs, your knees and thighs, up to your hips. Imagine them just sinking into the floor, heavy and relaxed.
5. Now think of your hands. Wiggle your fingers and flex your wrists, then let go, relax.
6. Think of your lower arm, elbow, and upper arm, all the way up to your shoulders. Picture all the tension just melting away.
7. Think about your abdomen. Let the tension go, and allow your breathing to flow more smoothly and deeply.
8. Think about your stomach and chest, up to your throat and neck. As you continue breathing more deeply, just imagine all the tension flowing out and you are relaxing more and more.
9. Now think about your throat, neck, and head, feeling limp and relaxed. Relax your facial muscles. Drop the jaw, parting the lips and teeth. Picture yourself completely relaxed.
10. If you are aware of any remaining tension anywhere in the body, go to the area mentally and relax the tension.
11. Continue to remain in this completely relaxed state for five to ten minutes. You may picture pleasant thoughts, or simply blank your mind and enter a stage of light sleep.
12. When you are ready to awaken, say to yourself, "I have been deeply relaxed. I am now ready to wake up, feeling completely refreshed and relaxed."
13. Begin to wake up by flexing the ankles, wiggling the toes. Then wiggle the fingers, and gently shake your wrists.
14. Bend the right knee, and then the left knee. Bend the right arm, then the left arm.
15. Open your eyes. Stretch each arm over your head. Then slowly sit up, stand up, and stretch again. You are ready to continue with your activities.

Three-Minute Relaxing Exercise

Often it is necessary to find the most expedient means to relax during high stress situations. The following is an example of a *short* relaxation exercise that is beneficial on a daily basis. This exercise is not to take the place of deep muscle relaxation but can be used in addition, to provide some feelings of general relaxation and to prevent headaches or other physical symptoms. This exercise can be used anywhere or any time you have three minutes (A good use of transition time between activities, appointments or projects! Great for traffic jams or commuter trains, too!):

1. *Interrupt your thoughts.* Stop thinking about your surroundings and switch your thoughts to your breathing. Take two deep breaths from your abdomen and exhale slowly. As you are exhaling, say to yourself: "I am becoming very relaxed."
2. *Scan your body for tense or uncomfortable areas.*
    a) With the power of your mind's eye, look for any tension in your calves, thighs and buttocks. Release any tension you find.
    b) Now, use your mind's eye to search out any tension in your stomach, chest and back. Simply let any tension you find flow gently out of your body with the next breath.
    c) Again, with the power of your mind's eye, try to detect any tension that may be in your shoulders, neck, jaws, eyes or forehead. Let any tension melt away as warm ripples of relaxation flow from the top of your head to your feet.
3. *Concentrate for fifteen seconds on warming your hands.* Feel the warm waves of relaxation flowing freely to your fingertips, making them warmer and warmer.
4. *Pick a pleasant thought, image, memory, or feeling.* Remain with it for a few seconds.
5. *Take another deep breath and return to your activities.*

Leisuring Your Way to Less Stress

Almost without exception, books, articles and experts in stress management place heavy emphasis on breathing and relaxation as two of the most effective avenues for reducing stress. The explanation for the beneficial effects of these techniques lies in the body-mind connection. Your body functions and well-being are directly influenced by what you do with your mind. Helping and then allowing your mind to become calm, uncluttered, peaceful, and passive will have a beneficial effect on your body and your lifestyle. Try the suggestions for breathing and relaxation in this chapter. You may be surprised at this new dimension of leisure!

Commercial Relaxation Aids

Several relaxation aids are now available commercially. These products are designed to help produce the deep relaxation we have described here. While we make no claims about their effectiveness, we believe the following items are worth telling you about (prices are current in Spring 1982):

- *Psychology Today* offers *instructional* cassette tapes. Two good ones are Deep Relaxation (#20034) and Meditation (#20033). They currently (1982) cost $9.95 each and can be ordered from *Psychology Today* Cassettes, Dept. A0410, P.O. Box 278, Pratt Station, Brooklyn, NY 11205. Ask for their FREE cassette catalog. (The cost per tape is 15% less when ordering four or more.)
- Some favorite *music* tapes are produced and distributed by HERU Records, P.O. Box 954, Topanga, CA 90290. Suggested titles:
  Seapeace ($8.98 cassette; $8.98 album). Georgia Kelly's first album. It is basically harp music that gently combines Eastern and Western moods.
  Ancient Echoes ($8.98 cassette; $8.98 album). Steven Halpern and Georgia Kelly combine their talents of harp, flute, keyboards and voice into eleven selections of many different but relaxing moods.

18

Stress Relief: Eating Habits

Ah, food! The great universal tranquilizer—or so it often seems. Actually, *good* nutrition *can* be a way of reducing stress, but, unfortunately, we tend to eat the wrong things. The result: *more* stress, not less. In this chapter, we'll take a look at why.

Because the field of nutrition is complex, and because there is so very much misinformation published and discussed about the relative values of various foods, we have chosen to rely heavily on two sources for the material in this chapter. The viewpoints which make most sense to us are those of the United States Senate Select Committee on Nutrition and Human Needs, chaired by Senator George McGovern (which issued its major report in 1977), and Jane Brody, whose *Nutrition Book* presents much authoritative information about the nutritive value of foods. You may disagree with these views, but *please* choose your experts carefully. And remember to use your own common sense! No one has yet disproved the value of a good "old fashioned" *balanced diet*!

Eating Your Way to Stress

Several major components of the typical American diet are, in the unfortunate proportions we usually consume them, potentially more harm than good. Sugar, for example, is one of those which can be a major contributor to stress.

It surprised us to learn that approximately 25% of the average American diet consists of refined sugars. And another 40% is loaded with fats. Although both sugar and fat do provide certain limited nutritional elements for our bodies, we consume on the average far more than we need for optimum health—and that is the problem.

In 1977, Senator McGovern's Committee on Nutrition recommended significant reductions in sugar, salt, fat and cholesterol consumption. They hoped to minimize some major health problems already linked at that time to excess quantities of these substances in the American diet. Their concerns included heart disease, cancer of the colon and breast, strokes, high blood pressure, obesity, diabetes, arteriosclerosis and cirrhosis of the liver.

If you are beginning to think that the average American eating habits can be a disaster—you are beginning to get the picture! But how do we *know* what to eat or what to avoid? Are there areas of a diet which are more harmful than others? Where should you begin? When the "experts" cannot agree, how are we to make our own way through the maze?

One sensible way is to *slowly* start changing those eating habits it has taken you years to form. Try alternative food products. Try unprocessed, fresh foods. Experiment with new ways of preparing and serving dishes. *Gradually* reduce the more harmful items and just as gradually increase the use of healthier foods. Consistency is important. As you begin to change and learn more about nutrition, other modifications will seem appropriate.

You should become aware of four areas of your diet which, if they are present in excess, can cause the most potential harm over the years: CAFFEINE, SUGAR, SALT, and FAT. Overconsumption of these four (…and most Americans do!)

can lead to potentially dangerous illnesses and trigger physiological reactions which are very similar to some of the reactions in a stress response (Chapter 1). Life usually produces enough situations that can result in anxiety, tension and stress. Doesn't it seem just a little unusual, maybe even crazy, to be eating your way to *more* stress?

The Great American Stress Break

Several times each day millions of Americans unknowingly create unnecessary stress responses in themselves. The irony is that these people are involved in a national ritual that is supposed to produce both mental and physical relaxation: the "coffee break."

The 10 to 15 minute break from work is a fairly standard morning and afternoon ritual. The most common ingredients include coffee or tea, a light "energizing" snack of pie, cake, rolls, candy bars, cookies, salted peanuts or chips. It is not uncommon for a cigarette to appear sometime during the break. The only thing wrong with that is...EVERYTHING! Despite minor variations, the ingredients usually include *caffeine, sugar, salt, and nicotine.*

Caffeine is a stimulant drug. In moderate amounts it can exhilarate, energize, and increase alertness and performance of many motor skills. The effects are normally felt within 30 minutes and will last for about three hours. In excessive amounts, however, caffeine can cause sweating, nervousness, jumpiness and anxiety. It also increases the secretion of stomach acids, reduces levels of blood sugar resulting in hunger pangs, leads to sleeplessness, could cause headaches, heartburn, heart disease, bleeding ulcers and possibly cancer of the bladder and pancreas.

Coffee is the most common source of caffeine, but not the only one. Most carbonated soft drinks, tea and chocolate contain caffeine. Consider the following chart and keep in mind that intakes of more than 250 mg per day are considered excessive.[*]

---

[*]Greeden, J.F. "Anxiety or caffeinism: A diagnostic dilemma." *American Journal of Psychiatry, 131,* 10, 1090 (October 1974).

ITEM	CAFFEINE CONTENT
*Excedrin (1 tablet)	65 mg
Soft drinks (12 oz)	32 - 65 mg
Coffee (5 oz)	66 - 146 mg
Tea (5 oz)	20 - 46 mg
Cocoa (5 oz)	13 mg
Chocolate candy (1 oz)	20 mg

Sources: *Journal of the American Dietetic Association, American Journal of Psychiatry*

*Source: Product label

Analyze your caffeine consumption. Is it excessive? What is your body telling you when you have too much? Slowly start decreasing your intake level until it is consistently below 250 mg per day. If you want to give up caffeine, investigate decaffeinated coffees (*some* have recently been suggested to contain carcinogens!), non-coffee grain beverages, name-brand herbal teas and juices. Read labels carefully and give your body time to wean itself from this drug.

The typical stress response affects your whole body from pituitary to pulse rate. Stress is usually caused by an atypical situation: waking up late, a dead battery, an IRS audit letter, a near traffic accident, a quarrel, a raise, a new job. A stress reaction can be beneficial and helpful in an emergency. The chemistry of your body creates an internal force that can continue helping you as long as you need to cope with the life event. But a stress response unknowingly and artificially created by the "Great American Coffee Break"—more appropriately called the "Great American Stress Break"— is of more harm than benefit. When compared to the standard stress response, the effects of caffeine and its common companions sugar and nicotine, can produce high levels of tension and anxiety—and very little renewal when you return to work after your "break"!

The Sugar You Did Not Know You Bought

In the late 1800's, Americans consumed an average of 40 pounds of sugar per person per year. Seem like a lot? It is, especially when you consider that sugar is an "empty" food which provides calories but does little nutritionally for your body. Vitamins, minerals, fibers and protein are virtually absent. Speculate about the *current* per capita sugar consumption while we tell you more about sugar.

The only good thing that can be said about sucrose (the chemical name for refined sugar, brown sugar, and honey) is that it provides a quick source of energy. Your body converts the sucrose into a simpler substance known as glucose which is the real source of the fast energy. In addition, glucose is converted into glycogen, a source of future energy which is stored in the muscles and liver until needed. But the quick energy of sugar is not such a great benefit. Other foods such as fresh fruits, fresh vegetables, whole grain breads and cereals, pasta, and dried beans and peas can provide the same energy levels as sugar. What's more, their contributions are of sustained value. Sugar's quick pick up disappears as fast as it comes. Even more important, these foods supply vitamins, minerals, and fibers; sucrose does not.

Not only is sucrose of little *use* to the body, when consumed in "typical American diet" excess it can be *harmful*. The most obvious problem is that a high intake of sugar results in a lot of calories. If the calories are not "burned" through physical activity, they are stored as fat and obesity can result. Consumption of both refined and natural sugars in excessive quantities has been linked to tooth and gum problems, raised levels of blood fats, kidney irregularities, blood pressure fluctuations and insulin imbalances. For those whose bodies have trouble processing sugar, it can lead to diabetes and increased blood cholesterol levels. In addition, since vitamin B complex is required to change carbohydrates into glucose, and since sugar does not contain any vitamins, the body must rob vitamin B from other sources. That can cause system-wide depletions if large quantities of carbohydrates are consumed. Such a vitamin deficit may, in turn, lead to anxiety, irritability and nervousness, particularly if one's usual diet is not adequate in the critical vitamins and other nutrients.

If other foods can provide the benefits without undesirable side effects—why would anyone continue to stress the body by eating sugar? The American diet is partially to blame. Sugar has become more widely used since the turn of the century. Now the average yearly consumption of sugar is —are you ready—*125 pounds,* with children gobbling up closer to *140 pounds*!

The amount of sugar we consume has dramatically increased partly because of commercial food processing methods. It is very difficult to find any type of commercially-prepared food that does not contain sugar. It is also present in so many tempting and habit-forming goodies such as jams and jellies, candies, gums, cakes, cookies, pies, custards, cobblers, puddings, syrups, toppings, ice creams, sherbets, donuts, sundaes, milk shakes and on and on. Many find it hard to imagine an all-American meal without a dessert of at least one of these items.

The hidden sugars in our "processed diet" make it hard to stay away from sugar even if you *want* to! Sugar is not only used in sweet baked goods but also in soft drinks, almost all fruit drinks, some baby foods, salad dressings, canned and dehydrated soups, frozen vegetables, most canned and frozen fruits and breakfast cereals. If you eat a hotdog, there is sugar in the meat, catsup, relish, mayonnaise, mustard, bun and even the chili if you go all the way!

Breakfast cereals are a real shocker. A study of 78 brands was reported in the *Journal of Dentistry for Children.*[*]

---

[*]American Society of Dentistry for Children, Sept./Oct., 1974, p. 18.

Shredded Wheat had the lowest with only 1% sucrose content. The percentages rose to a high of 68%! The sugar content of candy ranges from 39% to 97%. The average sucrose content of the dry cereals was 25%. Eat a breakfast of pre-sweetened cereal, sweetened fruit juice, toast with jelly or a roll and the level of sugar in this critical meal could easily approach 30 to 40%.

Cutting down on sugar takes effort and vigilance. It also takes acquiring a new taste for the exciting natural sweetness already in foods. Read labels. You will be amazed at how many processed foods in your daily diet contain sugar—almost every one. Since ingredients are listed in the order of quantity used, the sooner sugar is listed, the greater the proportion used. Just as important, do not be misled by such listings as dextrose, glucose, maltose, fructose, lactose, galactose, levulose, corn syrup, honey, corn sugar, or molasses. All are forms of sugar.

With so much sugar already in your food, it is not practical or possible to totally eliminate the consumption of "empty" or unneeded sugar calories. But you can follow a few suggestions for cutting down.

- In place of sweet snacks or candy, substitute popcorn, raw vegetables or fruits for the munchies. It really helps if the vegetables are already cut up and stored in the refrigerator, readily accessible for quick snacking.
- Get in the habit of serving fresh fruit for desserts. If you must rely on canned or frozen fruit, choose those packed in water instead of sweet syrup.
- Instead of buying cakes, pies or cookies, make your own. Try reducing sugar in the recipe a little more each time you bake.
- Make dessert breads that contain little sugar but are loaded instead with nourishing ingredients like whole wheat flour, oatmeal, nuts, raisins or perhaps cranberries, orange peels or carrots.
- Reward children with attention, privileges, gifts, fruit, nuts—*not sweets!*
- If you put sugar in coffee or tea, gradually reduce the

amount you use until you become accustomed to not using it at all. (Then go to work on cutting down the coffee or tea itself!)
- Eliminate soft drinks from your diet. Try other refreshing drinks such as mineral water, unsweetened vegetable or fruit juices or distilled water with a twist of lemon, lime or orange.
- Purchase dry cereals that have less than 10% sugar (3 grams per 1 oz. serving) and use fresh or dried fruits to provide the sweet flavoring you may crave.
- Finally, remember that "sugar substitutes" are likely to be harmful to your body also. Saccharine, for example, has been shown to produce cancer in laboratory animals.

Salt Preserves Your Food But Not Your Body

Salt plays many roles. It enhances flavors, controls ripening and bacterial growth in cheese and fruit, and preserves fermented foods like pickles. Many canned and processed foods are washed or stored in brine.

The sodium provided by salt is a very necessary element for proper body functioning, as are dozens of other chemicals. But like those other chemicals, too much can be damaging. Your body does not need a large amount of salt. The Food and Nutrition Board of the National Academy of Sciences—National Research Council—considers 1,100 to 3,300 milligrams per day as safe and adequate.*

Most Americans consume two to three times as much sodium as they need: current estimates of daily sodium intake are between 2,300 and 6,900 milligrams. One teaspoon of table salt (sodium chloride) contains approximately 2,000 milligrams of sodium. Many foods contain enough sodium naturally to meet most daily requirements. The excess consumption occurs when foods are processed with salt, cooked with salt, and then more salt is added at the table.

---

*Food and Nutrition Board, *Recommended Dietary Allowances.* National Academy of Sciences, 1974. Also *Jane Brody's Nutrition Book,* page 203.

Some of the food processing ingredients which contain sodium are monosodium glutamate or MSG (flavor enhancer), sodium saccharin (sweetener), sodium phosphate (stabilizer and buffer), sodium citrate (buffer), sodium caseinate (thickener and binder) and sodium benzoate and sodium nitrate (preservatives). Some common additives, although usually used in small quantities, are also high in sodium and should be avoided whenever possible: soy sauce, Worcestershire sauce, catsup, pickles, olives, garlic salt, onion salt, celery salt, baking soda, baking powder and monosodium glutamate (meat tenderizer).

To make matters worse, many foods that do not taste salty may still contain large amounts of sodium. Different varieties of the same food product may contain less sodium naturally or as a result of different processing techniques.

In general, foods in their natural state contain very little sodium but still enough to meet human daily requirements. Frozen vegetables are usually processed without added salt. However, vegetables with added sauces, mushrooms or nuts are higher in sodium than the plain variety. Canned vegetables are usually packed in a salt solution. Salted or brined meats and fish are obviously higher in salt content than uncured forms. Even the water softener in your home is a hidden source: it substitutes sodium for the minerals in hard water.

Consider the chart on the following page, which lists some foods very high in sodium next to others which are comparable but have much less salt.

Why should you be concerned with the level of sodium in your diet? Try these three compelling reasons:

- You are probably like most Americans who consume too much salt every day.
- Most salt is "hidden" and results in unknown and high levels of salt consumption. A few manufacturers are beginning to list the levels of sodium in their products. However, there is currently no federal requirement, and many do not voluntarily comply with consumer requests.
- The most important reason for carefully monitoring and

Low Sodium Levels			High Sodium Levels		
Food	Serving	Sodium (milligrams)	Sodium (milligrams)	Serving	Food
Cheddar cheese	1 oz	176	457	4 oz	Cottage cheese (reg. & low fat)
Mozzarella	1 oz	106	528	1 oz	Grated parmesan
Natural swiss	1 oz	74	388	1 oz	Pasteurized swiss
Sardines	3 oz	522	5234	3 oz	Smoked herring
Raw shrimp	3 oz	137	1955	3 oz	Canned shrimp
Cooked lean beef	3 oz	55	1114	3 oz	Ham
Chicken breast	½ breast	69	220	1 slice	Beef bologna
Peanuts (unsalted)	1 cup	8	986	1 cup	Peanuts (dry roasted, salted)
Pecans	1 cup	1	1200	1 cup	Cashews (dry roasted, salted)
English walnuts	1 cup	3			
Pistachios	1 cup	6			
Green beans (frozen)	1 cup	7	326	1 cup	Green beans (canned)
Corn (fresh cooked)	1 ear	1	384	1 cup	Corn (canned, regular, whole kernel)
Mushrooms (raw)	1 cup	7	968	1 cup	Mushrooms (canned)
Green peas (fresh cooked)	1 cup	2	493	1 cup	Green peas (canned)
Tomato paste	1 cup	77	1498	1 cup	Tomato sauce
Garlic powder	1 tsp	1	1850	1 tsp	Garlic salt
			1152	1 cup	Beef broth (cubed)
Popcorn (plain)	1 cup	1	75	1 cup	Popcorn (oil, salted)

Source: U.S. Department of Agriculture, Bulletin 233, August 1980.

restricting sodium intake is because future health and life may depend on it. After years of consuming too much salt, the body's mechanism for maintaining proper levels gradually becomes less efficient. As more sodium is retained, more water is retained. Blood volume increases, gradually placing more and more strain on the arteries and heart. Blood pressure gradually rises in those susceptible to this silent killer. Hypertension and cardiovascular problems and early death could result.

The most harmful effects of excessive salt consumption do not show up for years. The medical community cannot predict who will be endangered by high sodium diets before the damage is done. This means it is up to each of us to accept the dangers of a high salt diet and start changing now.

The steps are easy and inexpensive:
- Become conscious of daily salt intake by reading labels and learning of the hidden sources of salt.
- Start to reduce and eventually eliminate the addition of salt in cooking and at the table.
- Learn to use herbs and spices in place of salt. Dry mustard, garlic powder, celery, celery powder and allspice are good examples. Depending on the food, a large number of other spices could be used in place of salt. An excellent resource is a booklet available through the American Heart Association: *Cooking Without Your Salt Shaker.*

The Fat of the Land

About 40% of the typical American diet consists of fats from such sources as meats, butter, eggs, whole milk and cheeses. The average American consumes from 6 to 8 tablespoons of fat each day, yet we need only *one* tablespoon for balanced nutrition—and sometimes not even that much. The McGovern Committee on Nutrition and Human Needs recommended a reduction in fat consumption to a level closer to 30%, at the maximum.

Not all dietary fats are dangerous, of course. The major

health concern is with those which tend to increase cholesterol levels in the blood stream. Cholesterol, a substance contained in animal fat and produced by your body, is an essential body chemical. It is used by your cells to produce sex hormones, vitamin D, strong cell membranes and the protective sheaths around your nerves. The liver produces over 1,000 milligrams of cholesterol each day to meet these needs. No additional cholesterol is needed, yet the average American diet dumps an additional 600 milligrams into the body! As this excess travels through the blood stream, it clings to the artery walls, gradually closing them off. After a number of years, excessive fat consumption takes its toll in the form of atherosclerosis, heart attacks and strokes.

Saturated fats are the major villain in this drama, since it is this group which contributes to increased blood cholesterol. Examples of saturated fats, which should be minimized, include butter, cheeses made with whole milk or cream, milk chocolate, coconut and coconut oil, egg yolks, lard, meat fats, whole milk, poultry fat and vegetable shortening. (One key to spotting and recognizing many undesirable saturated fats is that they will be firmer and more of a solid at room temperature.)

A second type, *monounsaturated,* are classified into a "neutral" category. These include avocados, cashews, olives and olive oil, peanut butter, peanuts and peanut oil.

The last type, *polyunsaturated* fats, actually decrease blood cholesterol levels: almonds, corn oil, cottonseed oil, fish, pecans, safflower oil, soybean oil, sunflower oil, walnuts, and most margarines, mayonnaises, and salad dressings (check the labels!).

The fat you consume is not the whole story, of course. Some recent studies have shown that it is not blood cholesterol levels alone that are of concern. More important, according to these reports, is the proportion of *high density lipoproteins* in the blood cholesterol. The lipoproteins improve the body's capacity to absorb harmful cholesterol.*

**Jane Brody's Nutrition Book,* pp. 64-66.

High density lipoprotein levels are improved by vigorous exercise, among other things.

Other research lays blame for high blood pressure and other stress-related health problems with smoking, obesity, inactivity, environmental conditions and other factors. It is clearly a complex phenomenon! Nevertheless, reduced fat consumption appears to be one important and relatively easy step one can take toward better health and reduced stress. We urge you to consider these suggestions for gradually learning to live with less fat:

- Trim excess fat from meats; skin poultry before cooking;
- Select fish, poultry, lean meats, dry beans and peas as your protein sources;
- Limit your consumption of eggs (yolks have the highest cholesterol content of any food);
- Prepare foods by broiling, baking or boiling rather than frying;
- Limit your intake of cream; substitute polyunsaturated oils for fat; use polyunsaturated vegetable margarine for butter; and replace whole milk with low fat or skim milk;
- Read labels carefully to determine both the amount and types of fat contained in foods.

Up in Smoke

Although not technically a *dietary* consideration, smoking has such clear effects on the body's stress levels that it deserves mention here.

Arteriosclerosis, bronchitis, emphysema, heart disease, high blood pressure, cancer of the lung, larynx, lip, oral cavity, esophagus, bladder and other urinary organs are caused by smoking. Cigarettes, cigars, and pipe smoking deplete the body of nutrients. Smoking blunts the ability to taste and smell. Other people are forced to breathe the dangerous gases, which permeate skin, hair, clothes and furniture. The nauseous odors are easily detected by non-smokers—but not by smokers.

Claims of smokers notwithstanding, smoking does not

relax the body; it is a physical stimulant. Any relaxation from smoking is psychological—and very temporary! The only good thing which can be said about the dangerous and expensive crutch is, "I have kicked the habit!"

As prior smokers, it is easy for us (the authors) to acknowledge that stubbornness and keen ability to make excuses usually keep smokers from stopping. Since the early 60's when the Surgeon General first reported on the dangers of smoking, a continuous stream of reports have confirmed the hazards in books, articles, research papers, films, television specials.

Organizations such as the American Lung Association, the American Cancer Society, the American Heart Association and the National Institutes of Health produce an abundance of excellent information for anyone needing to be convinced to stop. Millions have successfully kicked the habit on their own, gradually, "cold turkey," or with the help of others through clinics and programs. The help is available; the research facts and statistics are becoming more overwhelming. What's your excuse for continuing this high stress habit?

On a Personal Level

Nearly all of the data we have presented in this chapter are based on large-scale studies and interpretations of what is "good for" the average person. The toughest part of all of this is that *no one is an "average person"!*

A nutritional program which is optimum for *you* must take into account your age, sex, lifestyle, level of general health, physical activity, stress factors, temperament, any short-term illness, any chronic medical condition.
There is no way we can offer in this book a recommended diet or eating plan which will take all these factors into account for every reader! Thus we urge you carefully to examine your own unique combination of the factors we have discussed. Develop a systematic plan for improving the way food contributes to *reducing* your overall stress level!

19

Stress Relief: Physical Fitness

In managing stress more effectively and efficiently, you are able to achieve a new picture or inner self-image. Regular physical exercise will promote more vital physical health, more positive emotional states and more acute mental powers. The alternative to physical fitness is diminished physical capacity with age. If you finally decide to "get with the program," you may find that your "get-up-and-go" has "got-up-and-gone"!

Fatigue and loss of energy are usually the first lines of defense for bodies whose owners resist exercise. It makes sense; rest *is* an age-old prescription for exhaustion. But more often than not, increased rest alone does not dispel fatigue.

Research evidence shows that physical fitness can reduce the incidence of coronary disease, hypertension, overweight, boredom, depression, premature aging, lack of flexibility, poor musculature, mental tension and stress-related diseases.

The federal government has initiated programs for federal employees based on evidence that fitness leads to reduced employee mortality. Matter of fact, of the fifteen variables that contribute to someone's chances of suffering a heart attack:

PHYSICAL FITNESS

blood pressure	EKG reading	fibrindysians
activity level	pulmonary function	cigarette smoking
blood sugar	heredity	uric acid
triglycerides	weight	glucose tolerance
mood and coping style	diet	cholesterol

all but one (heredity) can be positively affected by exercising for 25 minutes a day!*

Studies which have compared exercise to a widely prescribed tranquilizer found that exercise was superior in relaxing and elevating the individual's mood without any drug side effects.

As a bonus, it turns out that exercise is as good for your mind as it is for your body! Everyday problems seem less important, you tend to eat less, need less sleep. In fact, the quality of life is improved all around!

Even though physical fitness requires as much dedication and consistency as nutrition and rest, your exercise program can really be enjoyable. However, a few words of caution: don't do too much too soon or you run the risks of injury, becoming discouraged and quitting. If you are over 35, pregnant, or have some type of illness, it is wise to check out your prospective exercise program with a physician. Don't forget to do some warm-up stretching before exercising. This will prevent muscle pulls and unnecessary soreness. Most books on fitness give detailed examples of warm-up stretches.

Getting Started

Among the best exercises to improve your cardiovascular system and improve endurance are bicycling, walking, running and swimming. Our recommendation is to start with walking for ten minutes every other day for two weeks,

---

*NASA study in *American Journal of Cardiology,* Vol. 30, pp. 784-790.

fifteen minutes every other day the third week, and twenty minutes four to five times the fourth week. Gradually increase your pace, so that you are walking rapidly after a week or two. This kind of physical effort will allow you to tune in to your own body (perhaps for the first time?). After each workout, do some stretching exercises, have a glass of fresh fruit juice, take a shower and you are ready for anything. You will begin to discover new attitudes, feelings of achievement, less tension and more energy.

Getting Serious

- Discover what activity you do best. Analyze your body structure, environment, daily schedule, personal style, present physical condition.
- Find your own type of play. When exercise becomes play, it becomes a self-renewing habit. Look at your old skills from the earlier times in your life. How have you played before?
- Take a look at what your community has to offer: health club programs, local college classes, Y activities, public recreation facilities.
- Get a friend or group of friends involved (but don't stop yourself if others won't join you!).
- Read up on various physical activities (see the "Suggested Readings" section).
- Make physical fitness a regular, routine part of your life. Reassess your lifestyle if you think you are "too busy." (We submit that you cannot afford *not* to take the time!)
- Don't think of fitness as a crash program. Go slowly and gradually.
- Fitness should be fun; don't cheat yourself by taking any physical activity *too* seriously. Competition can give you *more* stress! Don't have heroic expectations for yourself.
- A valuable side benefit of exercise: you'll get in touch with Mother Nature. Exercise can be a good way to commune with the environment, sunsets, sunrises, flowers along the way, more time outside.

- A little activity goes a long way, so don't go overboard. Once you are "in shape," three 20-minute sessions a week can maintain a good level of fitness for you, if the activity produces sustained cardiovascular effort.
- Learn to breathe correctly as you are exercising.
- Express your fitness objectives in a contract with yourself; set daily, weekly, and monthly goals.

Physical Fitness Target *

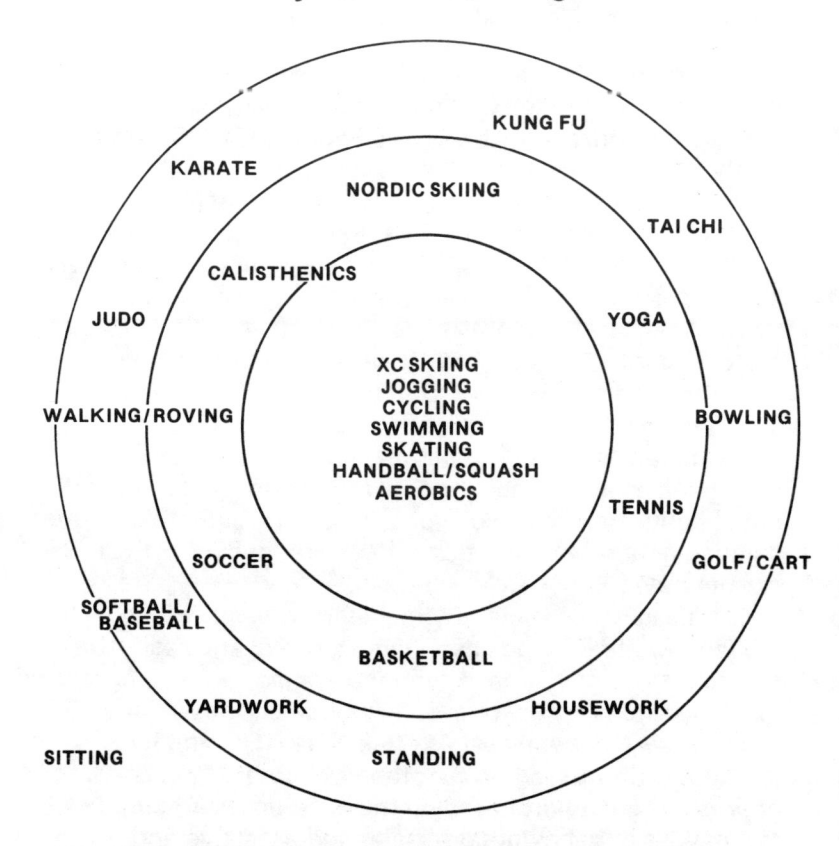

Innermost circle:
XC SKIING
JOGGING
CYCLING
SWIMMING
SKATING
HANDBALL/SQUASH
AEROBICS

Middle circle: NORDIC SKIING, CALISTHENICS, YOGA, TENNIS, BASKETBALL, SOCCER

Outer circle: KUNG FU, KARATE, TAI CHI, JUDO, WALKING/ROVING, BOWLING, GOLF/CART, HOUSEWORK, YARDWORK, SOFTBALL/BASEBALL

Outside circles: SITTING, STANDING

Those sports within the center have the greatest positive effect on your cardiovascular system. The farther from the center the activity is placed, the less the effect.

*Developed by Judy Pray, Laramie County Community College, Cheyenne, WY.

20

Stress Relief: Assertiveness and Time Management

Be Assertive with Stress!

Remember E.U. Stress and D.I. Stress back in Chapter 2? "D.I." was the person who couldn't handle the late alarm clock, and had trouble all day as a result. "E.U." took it pretty much in stride, and managed a productive day anyway. Several of the steps "E.U." took to help deal with the situation could be called *assertive* actions.

You may already consider yourself to be assertive in most situations. Nevertheless, we urge you to give the material in this section careful attention, especially if your People Stress score (Chapter 3) is above 75.

Unresolved problems which nag and bother, such as D.I. Stress experienced, often result in increased tension—and more and more anxiety. If put off, something that would have been easy to handle may grow in seriousness and get out of hand. Resolving such problems early can allow greater enjoyment of other activities and leisure, and assertiveness is a big help.

All of us are assertive to some degree; we may be able to say what we feel, to be open, honest, direct and respectful of others' feelings; in other situations, we may allow *others* to make decisions for us, or even to violate our own rights. This is *non-assertive* behavior. At other times it can be too easy to speak out without regard for others' feelings. This is *aggressive* behavior. Learning the differences among these three types of behavior (assertive, non-assertive and aggressive) and in what situations to use each is a key to making life more eustressful.

On the next page, you will find a list of everyday situations which call for assertive action. As you read each, consider your own behavior under similar conditions. Such a self-examination will give you an idea of the types of situations in which you may choose to be more assertive, and therefore guide your improvement efforts.

The next step toward more eustressful living is to *be* more assertive. You can grow in this area through classes and workshops, or with the help of a number of excellent books. The "Suggested Readings" section lists several of the more helpful books on the subject.

Assertive behavior can appear deceptively simple, of course. We suggest, "Be assertive!" as if you could go right out and change your life. Actually, the process is more complex than that. It does take practice, and sometimes guidance from a qualified professional trainer and/or a comprehensive self-help book. We suggest you check out *any* assertiveness training program to be sure it offers help—or referral—in four areas:

...*attitudes and thoughts.* Your belief system, ways of looking at life, and thoughts about yourself are important elements of your personal effectiveness.

...*behavioral skills.* Do you listen well? Do you look at others while talking? Do you stand erect? How is your timing? All these skills and others can make all the difference!

...*anxiety.* Anxiety and tension can prevent or distort effective communication, even if your attitudes and skills are right on target.

...*external obstacles.* Many life circumstances inhibit assertion. It's tougher to be firm with a boss when jobs are scarce, for example.

Achieving greater control in your life is a key dimension of stress management. Even if you consider yourself assertive already, there may be specific areas of your life which cause you difficulty and stress. We encourage you to read at least one of the recommended books on assertive behavior, and consider its potential value in helping to reduce your stress.

ASSERTIVENESS IN EVERYDAY SITUATIONS

- If a couple near me in a theater or at a lecture were conversing loudly, I would say something to them.
- If a salesperson has gone to considerable trouble to show me merchandise which is not quite suitable, I still say "no."
- I like to learn new games and skills.
- I am comfortable talking to attractive persons of the opposite sex.
- If a famed and respected lecturer made a statement that I thought was incorrect, I would share my view with the audience.
- I am comfortable making phone calls to businesses and institutions.
- I am open and frank in expressing my feelings.
- If something I buy is not suitable, I return it.
- When I do something important or worthwhile, I share my feelings of pride with others.
- When a close relative annoys me, I express my annoyance to that person.
- If I knew someone was spreading false stories about me, I would talk to that person about it.
- If someone pushed ahead of me in line, I would say something to that person.
- I complain when I get poor service or bad food in a restaurant.
- I ask friends to do favors for me.
- I express my feelings even when it may "make a scene."
- I am comfortable starting conversations with new acquaintances and strangers.
- If a friend borrowed $10 from me and forgot about it, I would remind the person to pay me back.
- I am comfortable asking questions in a group or class.
- When someone asks me to do something that I don't want to do, I say "no."
- I consider my own feelings equally important to those of others.
- I am able to enjoy rest and leisure.
- I know my needs are as important as the needs of other people.
- I consider making mistakes alright.
- I can ask for information from others, especially professionals.

The Time of Your Life: Friend or Foe?

Time management is concerned not with *how much* time you have (you have all there is!) but with how you *use* your time. Improving your time utilization allows you to avoid crises and thus stress, gain a feeling of accomplishment, and to live life effectively, not just spend it.

Time use strategy involves investigating and answering two important questions: "Where does my time go?" and "How can I use my time better?" It may take a little time to do this, but not as much as you might think. The time you save will be well worth it.

- In answering the first question ..

Devise a simple time log to keep a record of how your time is spent or wasted, hour by hour for a one-week period. Don't procrastinate until that "typical week" arrives; start now! After the week is over, categorize your time into work, leisure, people, sleep, and maintenance (eating, errands, bathing, chores, dressing). Make up your own categories to fit your lifestyle if that is more helpful. Finally, add up the hours in each category. Is this really the way you want to spend your life?

- Better use of your time is a tougher question...

Control of your time starts with planning on a daily basis and setting priorities. Then you can give up feeling guilty about lost opportunities and tasks undone. For example: If you are spending too much time in housework or yardwork, ask yourself if it might be more worth your time and money to pay a neighborhood boy or girl (or your own children) to do it for you. If you are finding that you are doing office work at home in the evenings and weekends and do not have enough time with the family, concentrate on incorporating more effective time management techniques at work.

Look at the way you are wasting your time. Check out "Interruptions" in the index of *How to Organize Your Work and Your Life*. You probably will find that you waste your time in similar ways every day. Many people discover that they are their own worst time wasters. If so, remember it is easier to be assertive with *yourself* and change *your* habits rather than someone else's!

If procrastination is a primary time waster for you, begin to conquer it. Don't let "trying to be super perfect" paralyze you. If you decide to put everything off until it is definite, you'll get nothing done. Make it a practice not to avoid the most difficult problems. That will just insure that the hardest part will be left when you are the most exhausted!

Different people respond better to different time schedules. Perhaps you are a "morning person" and function best between 6 and 9 a.m.; don't expect everyone to function effectively at that time. Find out when you are your "superself" and plan your most important activities during that time. The time log can help you find your best time. When you find it, don't waste your best energy and time with trivia which can wait until you are not your most productive.

Start with only one task at a time. At work, try to avoid clutter on your desk or workbench—it is distracting. After you have chosen a task, follow it through to the finish whenever possible...even if you have to delay lunch. Then you avoid having to reacquaint yourself with those loose threads.

Control of your time starts with planning on a daily basis and setting priorities. Then you can give up feeling guilty about lost opportunities and tasks undone. Here is a suggested list of time savers. They won't *cure* your "clock pains," but they will help you manage your most valuable resource!

Ninety-Five Ways to Save Time *

At Home...
Keep a bulletin board (with appointment calendar attached) near the phone.

---

*Reprinted from the May/June 1981 issue *Women in Business*. The national publication of the American Business Women's Association. Used by permission.

Schedule play time on your calendar so you will be sure to relax, create, exercise and be with friends regularly.

File coupons and other papers in file boxes to maintain clean bulletin boards and desk tops.

Use family or group time to brainstorm ideas for menus, vacation plans or new ways to budget.

Put an asterisk beside each tax-deductible expenditure on your monthly budget sheet or in your checkbook. At tax time, simply transfer the items to one sheet.

Pay a tax accountant to do your income tax.

Keep a notebook in your car glove compartment for noting service and maintenance dates.

Walk straight from your mailbox to the trash can to deposit junk mail.

Put things away after using them.

Make meals ahead of time and freeze them to use on heavy-schedule days.

Hire a high school student to do yard work.

Plan an energy renewal at least once a week in the form of a yoga lesson.

Learn to say "no" and mean it.

Lay out things you'll need the night before.

Learn to do nothing as a way of calming your mind and body.

Train children and friends to respect your quiet time and thank them often for that.

Arrange for your bank to do as much of your banking as possible by mail and phone (e.g., ordering new checks by phone; automatic processing of savings deductions from paychecks).

Have an automatic reply for door-to-door salespeople.

Ask friends to help you find a job, service or product; establish an information network.

Get rid of your television set.

Take time to eat and sleep properly.

Keep a shopping list on your bulletin board so that you can jot down needs as they develop.

Obtain all major department store catalogs, compare prices, and shop by telephone.

Make a list of errands which can be done in the same shopping center or area of town so that you save time and gas by a one-trip consolidation.

Plan all doctor appointments for the same day (e.g., gynecologist, eye doctor, dentist).

Read the food specials so you can stock up on staples by the case.

Purchase and use a grocery item adder or mini-calculator for shopping to assess the total before reaching the check-out counter.

Use waiting time at the laundry or auto repair shop to go to the library, shop, read or write letters.

Buy two books of stamps at a time to avoid continually running out.

Refuse to buy cars, furniture or other items needing babying or special care.

Buy simple, easy-to-maintain clothing which can be laundered. Give up ironing.

At Work...
Place a large planning calendar on the wall so you are aware of key meetings and deadlines.

Carry a small appointment calendar to record appointments as they are made.

Keep a small notebook or index cards with you for writing down ideas as they occur.

Plan time several months in advance for ongoing priority projects.

Give yourself deadlines for assignments and tasks.

Schedule breakfast and lunch meetings instead of evening meetings.

When holding meetings, allow participants to come and go as their contribution is needed and completed. It is not always necessary for everyone to stay at the meeting for the entire time.

Open your mail in the latter part of the morning or in the afternoon instead of at 9:00 a.m. There is always a variety of items in the mail, and these varied items diversify your thoughts away from your top priority items.

Pull files or other material before you leave the office.

Maintain an "interruption" log for analysis.

Limit your attendance at meetings.

Go through paperwork only once.

Go through your past correspondence and find your best paragraphs on every common subject that normally occurs in your writing. Compile them all into a loose-leaf binder, organized by subject and number each paragraph. Give a copy to your typist. To create new correspondence, just leaf through your book until you find the paragraph you want to use. Use the code numbers in the order you want them typed.

Use written communication or telephone conference calls in place of meetings.

Delegate your attendance at meetings to subordinates.

Hold stand-up meetings if possible.

Set target dates for completion of every project.

Save all the paper trivia for a three-hour session once a month.

Clear your desk of all projects except the one at hand.

Learn to develop an intense concentration span for everything you do.

Send post cards instead of letters or making phone calls.

Make a list of things which can be done in five minutes or less. Whenever you have a few minutes and don't know what to do, go over your short-task list.

Designate a place for everything and keep it there.

Set priorities for your first concerns each morning and attend to them one by one.

Don't schedule meetings for the sake of meetings.

Prepare meeting agendas and stick to them.

Concentrate on only one thing at a time to avoid fragmentation.

Stop shuffling through papers, avoiding decisions; handle each paper only once.

Ask yourself: "How could I best spend this moment?"

Don't waste the time of other people or intrude on their quiet periods.

Avoid negative people who sap you of energy and who have a "can't do" approach to the world and their work.

Stay in touch with enthusiastic people who motivate you by their productivity and zest for life.

Know when you have reached your peak of efficiency and stop when you feel tired.

Spend less time on the phone.

Train yourself to cut down on coffee breaks, trivial conversation, and other time wasters during office hours.

Eat a simple, sustaining lunch to prevent afternoon grogginess.

Respond to letters on the original letter; photocopy that and file it.

List tomorrow's priorities before leaving the office today.

If someone asks, "Have a minute?" say "no" if you don't.

Arrange your office with back to door.

If you can, have all calls screened. List who should be put through.

Set time limits for meetings.

Travel...
Keep a list of items to pack taped inside your suitcase lid for hasty departures.

If you are frequently away overnight, keep a tote bag packed with the following items: deodorant, soap, toothbrush and paste, curlers, makeup, razor, nail polish and remover, extra traveler's checks, coins for stamps, soft drinks, tips or parking.

Use airport waiting time to read or write letters.

Utilize long commuting trips for dictating correspondence, or studying language by cassette.

Carry a crushable, all-purpose suitcase aboard the airplane to avoid checking and awaiting baggage.

Relationships...

Assess how much time a relationship will require before leaping into it.

Deal with resentments or bad feelings as soon as you recognize them to preclude hours of wasted time fretting.

Spend more time with people who really matter to you.

Decompression

Sound like a SCUBA diving technique to avoid physical distress? Actually, it is a type of time management technique which helps you keep the distress in one area of your life from spilling over into and contaminating other areas.

It's a classic story: Carolyn (or Carl) was so angered at work that she ran people off the road on the way home, slammed the door on the way into the house, screamed at the innocent and bewildered children, and kicked the dog (a great example of raw, inexcusable aggression).

We all need to be able to let down in a healthy, controlled way and thus "decompress" after one activity before going on to the next. It is especially important to decompress between work and home, but you should also do it between demanding activities throughout the day so you can be your most efficient, effective, and lovable self.

What will work? ALMOST ANYTHING! Look inside yourself at your needs. What helps you unwind? What helps you put something out of your mind? If it works, use it as long as it is healthy for yourself and others.

Some other basic principles about decompression to keep in mind: you need to want to do it; be specific about when and what you are going to do; have several options in case one does not feel right; vary the activity or technique from time to time; know about how much time it will take; don't work so hard at decompressing that you become more distressed trying! Finally, adopt an attitude that says *you deserve* the time to rejuvenate yourself. The time you take for yourself will provide you with more energy, more enthusiasm, and more productivity. Test it out, then believe and enjoy!

Over the years, we have assembled a collection of decompression techniques used by various people (including us). A word of caution: be open to the techniques. Many will need to be modified to fit your lifestyle:

- watch the evening news, read the newspaper or a magazine (for some, this in itself will cause more distress)
- open the mail (could also be distressful at times!)
- clean a room or a portion of a room
- take a 15-20 minute nap
- engage in physical activity
- share the ups and downs of the day, up to a maximum of 15-20 minutes, with spouse, children, a friend, a pet
- meditate or relax for a few quality minutes
- pray while you are driving home (don't close your eyes), as you fix supper, while you are relaxing, or anytime
- take a few minutes to mentally review the day; look forward to the evening or tomorrow; organize yourself for the next day; make a list of things to do
- get out of the house or into a quiet part of the house if possible, with the help of a spouse or friend, to do something special by yourself and for yourself
- have a cup or glass of your favorite non-alcoholic, non-caffeine drink
- take a quick or leisurely shower/bath (alone or with someone)
- take a leisurely or brisk walk after supper.

You have the idea. Almost anything will work. The worst thing you can do is to say you "do not have the time" to do anything to decompress. *Make the time!* You need to be good to yourself. You deserve it. If you don't do something to decompress and make a smooth transition from stressful situations, you will not be able to keep up the pace, physically or psychologically.

21

Stress Relief: Avoiding Burnout

Mention the word "burnout" and almost everyone within earshot will quickly admit — almost proudly — that they are experiencing it. Images abound: dying embers, smoldering wicks, and cold, gray ashes....

What does burnout have to do with stress? What are the causes and symptoms? Is it treatable?

Burnout And Stress

Burnout is linked to distress. Remember that stress is neutral; it only becomes "good" or "bad" from your reactions to it. Coping well results in eustress, which can be a motivator and energizer. Ineffective coping results in distress, which will eventually lead to physical and psychological problems. When distress is left untreated, burnout gradually sets in.

The People-Work Connection

Who is at risk of burning out? What happens on the job to lead to burnout? Everyone is susceptible, especially when a working environment deteriorates.

It is not the job itself which causes burnout. It is your personal negative reaction; even exciting and fun jobs can lead to disaster if you begin to care less and less about work and begin to seek more and more of your enjoyment and fulfillment from sources outside the job.

When you begin a new job, you are usually enthused, fired up, dedicated, full of energy, excited, willing to work hard. When this kind of good "fit" exists between you and your work, enthusiasm, satisfaction, productivity, achievement, and personal growth usually result. But when a poor fit either exists or develops over time, the job becomes less rewarding.

In time, job stagnation turns into frustration; major disappointments, unresolved problems, and irritations lead to impatience and intolerance. You may begin to question your effectiveness on the job — even the value of the job itself. Eventually, if no intervention occurs, you will probably become more and more apathetic. You punch in; you punch out, doing the bare minimum required to get by.

This is burnout; a total physical and emotional exhaustion combined with a sense of frustration, powerlessness, and apathy — all resulting from job distress.

Warning Signals

It doesn't happen in a flash, with lots of sparks and smoke. Usually, there are several telltale warning signals that something is smoldering. First, comes a gradual, progressive increase in emotional and physical exhaustion. The rest and replenishment so badly needed never come. Second, burnout is usually associated with *job* distress. Your reactions to the normal stresses of work can lead to stagnation, frustration, powerlessness, and apathy.

Everybody who works is susceptible. (A word of caution to homemakers and students: even though your work is nontraditional, you are just as much at risk as those in other occupations.) Finally, the distress on the job spills over eventually into the other areas of your life, resulting in burnout.

Your response to conditions at work (including organizational, environmental, and people stressors), despite its impact on your personal life, is not the whole story. You bring stressors to the job (people, work, money, leisure, mind, and body) which affect the work atmosphere. Your reaction to both sets of stressors, those from the job and those you bring to the job, interact to fuel the burnout process.

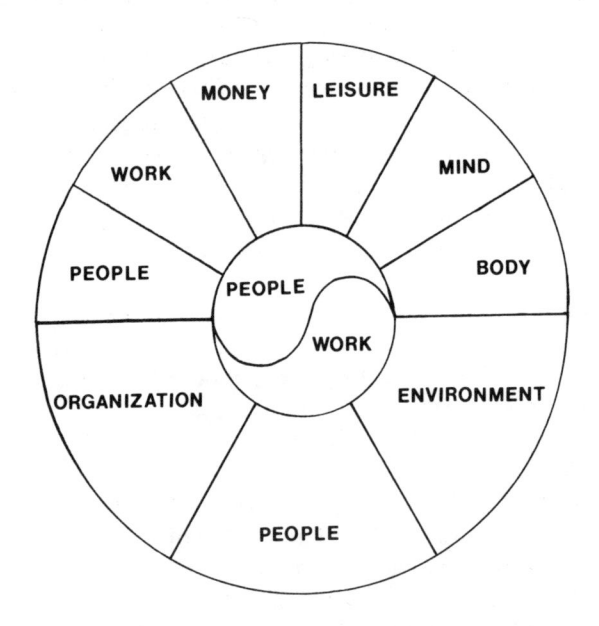

Since you and your job both contribute to burnout, you and your employer have a joint opportunity and responsibility to recognize the symptoms and deal with the issues before they become too serious. Employers and workers must point to themselves, not to each other, for causing the problem. At the same time, each must seek coping strategies and buffers which will prevent burnout before it starts, or relieve it if it exists.

Burnout is not terminal, usually. It is infectious, however, and can spread like wildfire through your personal and professional life if ignored. While everyone becomes singed around the edges at times from pushing too hard or ignoring the warning signs, burnout is treatable.

What is even more encouraging is that burnout is not inevitable. It can be prevented.

Burning Issues

You spent some important time in Chapters 3-8 finding out the specific stressors which created distress in your personal life. If left untreated these stressors can spill over into your job and increase your chances of burning out. Your job can also contribute unique factors which may lead from distress to burnout. Use the following list of potential work stressors as a checklist to assess your job situation. The more issues which exist, the more likely burnout could begin.

Organization
- Unclear or too many rules, regulations, or policies
- Poor management
- No career ladder available for employees
- No autonomy
- Frequent changes within the workplace without input from the people affected
- Unclear, changing, or lack of job descriptions
- Decisions constantly made by supervisors without input from employees
- Few external awards for a job well done
- Work overload, underload
- Overpromotion, underpromotion
- Absence of programs for employee renewal, training, or development

People
- Lack of cooperation among employees or departments
- Poor supervision
- Complaining and backbiting by employees
- Predominantly negative feedback from supervisors
- Lack of informal or formal staff meetings
- Lack of recognition by supervisors for good work
- Little or no faith, trust, or openness among staff members

Environment
- Poor communication within the workplace
- No freedom for creativity, mistakes, or differences of opinion
- Problems remain unresolved for long periods of time
- Employee stagnation (same office and/or responsibilities year after year)
- Office politics
- Distressful working conditions (lack of privacy, loud noises)
- Responsibility but no authority to carry out decisions

People Symptoms

A fever is a symptom of an infection in the body. Burnout also has some unique symptoms which can act as a warning if you know what to look for. The five sets of symptoms presented below begin with *physical* reactions and progress through the *spiritual*. Symptoms in all five areas seem to develop sequentially, but become progressively worse when all are present in your life.

How long does it take for someone to burn out? It can take a few months or a few decades. Many people never experience burnout. *You are more at risk any time you give in to the frustrations and give up trying to cope.*

The symptoms presented here are never all present in one person. Look for those which are most characteristic of your coping style. Look for symptoms in your coworkers. Be especially alert to the *physical* and *social* symptoms, because burnout is most easily treated at these stages. Yet the tendency is to ignore these symptoms. No one can ignore the (later) psychological and spiritual symptoms, as they destroy the individual and threaten the workplace. Everyone wants to help then, but by that time the victim may be very resistant, denying that a problem even exists. Early detection and prevention are the keys.

Physical Symptoms (Your body will be the first to go)
- extended fatigue and persistent tension
- feeling drained or used up
- difficulty sleeping, falling asleep, or feeling rested
- suffering from a generally poor physical condition
- maintaining poor eating habits and exhibiting weight changes
- increased potential for digestive disorders, lower back pains, and coronary problems

Social Symptoms (After your body goes, friends are not far behind)
- decreased importance of relationships
- increased irritability (you become a real grouch)
- having difficulty dealing with people: less patience, more resentment and anger, more tendency to lash out
- more complaints about work
- less time spent in pleasant conversations with family or friends
- putting off personal interactions both at work and at home
- a gradual preference for isolation
- reluctance to share feelings with spouse, friends, colleagues
- increased clock-watching
- diminished sense of humor

Psychological Symptoms (Now that your body and friends are gone, your mind is next)
- feelings of being overloaded with information and details
- beginning to avoid tasks that involve thinking
- finding it difficult, if not impossible, to concentrate
- problems on the job become more and more difficult to handle
- demonstrating inaccurate, poor judgement
- increased aggression and cynicism toward people
- curt and sarcastic responses to people
- setting unrealistic goals

- finding it difficult to go to work each day
- a tendency to stereotype colleagues and customers at work
- increasingly "going by the book"
- feelings of alienation from people and tasks
- deepening feelings of boredom
- missing deadlines with little or no remorse
- feeling like one is always meeting *someone else's* needs
- increasing levels of unexpressed anger and frustration
- increased suspicion, distrust, resentment
- feelings of helplessness and hopelessness
- mood swings
- overwhelming feelings of depression, pessimism, and failure
- use of drugs and alcohol as solutions

Spiritual Symptoms (When everything else is gone,...)
- seriously doubting one's own personal values and beliefs
- feeling threatened by others
- questioning your contributions to society, family, work
- impulsive and major changes in lifestyle (divorce, running away, quitting the job)
- experiencing feelings of emptiness, anxiety, disillusionment
- constantly looking for the easy solution or magic answer
- denying that a problem exists or blaming others for the problem
- rejecting all offers for help
- possible suicide attempts

Work Symptoms

When something goes wrong in the workplace, the word spreads and the organization, no matter how large or small, suffers and is weakened. One or two people may be in the process of burning out and the ripples will spread. Those who are burning out will be given more slack. Their symptoms will be ignored. Work begins to pile up, and staff members who are not victims become overloaded with the undone work.

Overloaded co-workers may express anger toward the burnout victims.

You can see what begins to happen. Eventually, the whole workplace can begin to burn out if no prevention or intervention takes place. It is very important to be able to recognize the symptoms in yourself, your colleagues, and your workplace, so you can do something about it.

Here are some typical symptoms of organizational burnout:
- a pattern of absenteeism evolves (i.e., increased use of sick days, extended lunches and breaks)
- high staff turnover rate
- complaints surface about performance — from colleagues, management, and the public
- lower motivation, lack of initiative
- higher frustration levels
- scapegoating organizational leaders
- depersonalized services and interactions
- avoidance of certain tasks or people
- declines in productivity, quality of work, service
- interdepartmental competition and friction
- rigid boundaries evolve between offices and departments
- staff roles and functions become fixed
- deadlines are missed
- declining level of efficiency, diminished interest in work
- persistent failure to perform required tasks
- increased conflicts with authority
- arbitrary decision-making
- acting-out behavior emerges (e.g., silent withdrawal, destructive criticism, raising irrelevant issues)
- unwillingness to engage in conflict-resolution or problem-solving
- backbiting, nitpicking, sabotage
- use of alcohol or other drugs on the job
- psychosomatic illnesses emerge (e.g., hypertension, ulcers, colitis, strokes, migraines, tension headaches).

Burnout Buffers

Hang in there! Burnout is treatable. The solutions lie in whatever will rekindle the flame for you. Remember, burnout symptoms are unique to each victim. Your burnout buffers must also reflect this individuality.

Your first step in learning to spark again is knowing and recognizing your own symptoms. After you have completed an analysis of your situation, do not wait to get started. Remember, the longer you allow yourself to suffer with burnout symptoms, the more difficult it will be to light your fire! Prevention is a key concept for coping with burnout, not only in yourself but also in the workplace. The buffers listed below are proven, effective techniques for organizations. Look them over carefully and, if necessary, modify them to fit your situation.

The dozens of buffers you reviewed in Chapters 11-16 are excellent resources for coping with burnout on a personal level, especially the Work Buffers. In addition, you may want to consider:

- accentuating the positive in your job (concentrating on accomplishment, conversing, sharing jokes, making positive feedback a personal commitment)
- developing transition time activities to decompress (see Chapter 20)
- personalizing your work environment with photos, paintings, flowers, sculptures, special calendars
- becoming involved in meaningful projects or committees which can bring variety to work
- evaluating the meaningfulness of your work tasks so you can determine where your personal investment of time and energy should be directed.

The organization, through its managers and supervisors, has some options which can relieve burnout symptoms. The symptoms must not be ignored because the more people feel burned out, the closer the entire organization comes to

snuffing the collective flames of productivity and job satisfaction. If you are in a position of power or influence, we urge you to consider:
- supporting innovation and creativity
- improving feedback to employees
- increasing employee participation in decisions that directly affect them
- when no compromise is feasible, clearly explaining why
- giving information to supervisors and other employees as problems arise
- developing realistic, complete job descriptions
- developing clearer, more positively stated policies and procedures
- establishing flexible leaves and support services
- improving training programs
- creating better divisions of labor
- changing standard operating procedures
- redesigning jobs
- rotating jobs
- designing and encouraging lateral job transfers
- encouraging team efforts with goal-setting, problem-solving
- suggesting and supporting cross-training
- modifying contacts with the public to reduce distress
- creating mentorships so that newly hired employees have a good orientation to the workplace, including job stressors
- limiting job spillover by discouraging overtime and encouraging breaks, lunch hours, and vacation time
- suggesting professional help (medical, psychological)
- modifying reward systems based on employee needs, desires
- changing management style, organizational structure
- offering stress management and time management training (the authors — and hundreds of other qualified consultants — are available!)
- providing career counseling
- limiting length of meetings

- creating evaluation procedures that provide positive feedback and opportunities for growth
- supporting creation of positive work environments
- celebrating personal and departmental successes, milestones, events
- building-in recreation and play time
- encouraging and rewarding individual efforts at physical fitness and wellness

Burnout Bibliography

Edelwich, Jerry. *Burn-Out: Stages of Disillusionment in the Helping Professions.* New York: Human Sciences Press, 1980.

Freudenberger, Herbert J. *Burn-Out: The High Cost of High Achievement.* New York: Bantam Books, 1980.

Maslach, Christina. *Burnout: The Cost of Caring.* Englewood Cliffs, NJ: Prentice-Hall, Inc., 1982.

Melendez, Winifred A. & Rafael M. deGuzman. *Burnout: The New Academic Disease.* Washington, D.C.: ASHE-ERIC, Higher Education Research Report No. 9, 1983.

Murphy, Dana H. (ed.). *Staff Burnout.* Rockville, MD: National Drug Abuse Center for Training and Resource Development, 1980.

Paine, Whiton S. (ed.). *Job Stress and Burnout: Research, Theory, and Intervention Perspectives.* Beverly Hills, CA: Sage Publications, 1983.

Pelletier, Kenneth R. *Healthy People in Unhealthy Places: Stress and Fitness at Work.* New York: Delacorte Press, 1984.

Pines, Ayala M. & Elliot Aronson. *Burnout: From Tedium to Personal Growth.* New York: The Free Press, 1981.

Veninga, Robert L. & James A. Spradley. *The Work-Stress Connection: How to Cope With Job Burnout.* New York: Ballantine Books, 1981.

Welch, I. David, Donald C. Medeiros, & George A. Tate. *Beyond Burnout.* Englewood Cliffs, NJ: Prentice-Hall, Inc., 1982.

A Footnote

The end of this book is only the beginning of your new discoveries in stress relief.

Stress has become a permanent by-product of our fast-paced, ever-changing world. As your lifestyle changes, your way of coping and finding relief will also need to change. Stress relief cannot be a "passing fad." It must be incorporated as a permanent way of living. When you need new stress buffers to meet new stresses, you can flip back through the covers of this book and make new discoveries. There are also many other good books and intensive training programs available for relaxation, nutrition, exercise, assertiveness, time management and other stress management strategies. Explore freely!

We leave you with a challenge: Be healthy and free of distress! It is a challenge you are prepared to meet with the skills you have learned in this book. You can make the choice to spend life, survive life or live life. CHOOSE WELL...

Suggested Readings

- Alberti, Robert and Emmons, Michael, *Your Perfect Right: A Guide To Assertive Living* (Fourth Ed.). San Luis Obispo, CA: Impact Publishers, Inc., 1982.

    The first book designed for the layperson interested in developing more assertive behavior. Contains a supplementary section on technical materials for the professional.

- Albrecht, Karl, *Stress and the Manager: Making It Work for You.* Englewood Cliffs, NJ: Prentice-Hall, Inc., 1979.

    This book contains a well-presented description of the stress concept. The author presents an analysis of "wellness" which is a good stimulus to learn more about holistic approaches to health.

- Ardell, Donald, *High Level Wellness: An Alternative to Doctors, Drugs, and Disease.* Emmaus, PA: Rodale Press, 1977.

    A guidebook to optimal well-being that tells you the things you need to know to shape a richly positive lifestyle that will keep you younger longer. The book includes self-tests you can use to determine your present level of wellness; ways to integrate the five dimensions vital to your health needs; strategies for shaping your personal environment to reduce fatigue, and lower stress.

- Abrahamson, E.M. and Pezet, A.W., *Body, Mind, and Sugar.* New York: Avon Books, 1977.

    Explains the extraordinary role that blood sugar plays and the mechanism that keeps body and mind in a healthy balance. Case histories show how low blood sugar can be misdiagnosed and, as a consequence, dangerously ignored. Also gives simple diets which have been used successfully in the treatment of sugar starvation. Note: low blood sugar is NOT treated by consuming more sugar!

- Ahl, David H. (Ed.), *Basic Computer Games.* New York: Workman Publishing, 1978.

    The computer programs in this book are written to run in Micro-Soft BASIC computer language. Over 90 complete programs are printed for literally months of fun or frustration, depending upon how good you are at the games. If you don't have a computer, many colleges and libraries are acquiring microcomputers for the public to use. Some already have games programmed. Check your local resources.

SUGGESTED READINGS

- Bach, George and Wyden, Peter, *The Intimate Enemy: How to Fight Fair in Love and Marriage.* West Caldwell, NJ: William Morrow & Co., Inc., 1969.

  How to fight fair in love and marriage. Fight: it's good for you! But fight fairly; untrained fighting can be dangerous. Under pressure, the temptation is strong to strike at weak points, throw in irrelevancies, and go for a "kill." This book demonstrates, with 122 real fights, the flexible rules and exercises for *fair,* above-the-belt fighting. These reduce insults and injuries and lead to increased understanding, growth, and job satisfaction.

- Bach, George and Deutsch, Ronald, *Pairing.* New York: Avon Books, 1975.

  Achieve genuine intimacy in marriage: understand first impressions, detect and prevent exploitation, reduce fears of rejection, establish genuine intimacy, and appreciate the value of conflict.

- Bammel, G. and Burrus-Bammel, Lei Lane, *Leisure and Human Behavior.* Dubuque, IA: William C. Brown Co., 1982.

  For anyone interested in a comprehensive, easily read and fascinating view of American leisure behavior. Discusses leisure from the perspective of play, time, games, work, theories, current practices, and even career opportunities. Especially recommended for the professional who works with people or anyone needing to be convinced of the legitimacy of leisure.

- Bartz, Wayne and Rasor, Richard, *Surviving with Kids: A Lifeline for Overwhelmed Parents.* San Luis Obispo, CA: Impact Publishers, Inc., 1978.

  "A jargon-free practical book for parents." Thirty proven principles of behavior applied to parent-child interaction. Clearly written, down-to-earth and illustrated with cartoon-style examples of everyday situations.

- Benson, Herbert, *The Relaxation Response.* NY: Avon Books, 1976.

  Synthesis of modern discoveries and religious/philosophic literature regarding the effects of meditation techniques. Benson describes how to deal constructively with the pressures of contemporary society through a meditation technique he calls the "relaxation response."

- *The Bible* (choose from the wide range of excellent versions).

- Bolles, Richard, *The Three Boxes of Life and How to Get Out of Them.* Berkeley, CA: Ten Speed Press, 1978.

A very easy-to-read book filled with lots of interesting cartoons, charts, and flair. It is an introduction to life/work planning which helps you look at education, work, and retirement. The book deals with all three at once, what's wrong with them, what could be right with them, and how you might do something about them in your own life...now. The emphasis is on blending learning (education), achievement (work), and leisure (retirement) during *all* the stages of your life.

- Bolles, Richard, *What Color Is Your Parachute?* Berkeley, CA: Ten Speed Press, 1982.

Job-hunters and career-changers will appreciate this very practical manual. It tells you in step-by-step detail how to identify what you want to do with the rest of your life, how to locate the job you want, and how to convince the employer you are the best person for the job. Includes the "Quick Job-Hunting Map" which is a very useful and necessary tool in helping you eventually decide what you want to do with your life.

- Boston Women's Health Collective, *Our Bodies, Ourselves: A Book by and for Women.* NY: Simon & Schuster, Inc., 1976.

This book is the encyclopedia of self-responsibility for women. It is designed to help women to understand, accept, and be responsible for their own health and well-being.

- Bower, Sharon and Gordon, *Asserting Yourself: A Practical Guide for Positive Change.* Reading, MA: Addison-Wesley Publishing Co., 1976.

A practical, complete, step-by-step program for becoming more assertive. Important skills for improving self-esteem, coping with stress, and making more friends. Describes DESC scripts, a new technique for dealing with all kinds of interpersonal conflict. Lots of exercises, examples, and ways to change.

- Brody, Jane, *Jane Brody's Nutrition Book.* NY: W.W. Norton & CO., 1981.

This is probably the soundest and most comprehensive guide to nutrition yet available for the layperson. The 27 chapters cover in detail, yet in understandable language, every aspect of nutrition from the basics of essential nutrients to reading food labels. This book is more than facts; it is a way of increasing nutrition awareness. A real pleasure to read and use.

- Brown, Barbara, *Stress and the Art of Biofeedback.* NY: Bantam Books, 1977.

The author, one of the best authorities on biofeedback, provides a comprehensive explanation of how the technique of biofeedback has been used to successfully treat more than 50 major stress-related disorders.

- Buxbaum, Robert and Micheli, Lyle, *Sports for Life: Fitness Training, Injury Prevention and Nutrition.* Boston, MA: Beacon Press, Inc., 1979.

Twenty popular sports are analyzed including aerobic dancing, hiking, and running.

- Campbell, Greg, *The Joy of Jumping.* NY: Richard Marek Publishers, Inc., 1978.

The world's fastest human with a jump rope outlines his complete jump rope program for health, looks, and fun. Teaches "the perfect exercise," and offers a program which requires virtually no time (5 to 10 minutes and *not* every day), money, space, sweating, or pain(?).

- Chadwick, Janet, *How to Live on Almost Nothing and Have Plenty.* NY: Alfred A. Knopf, Inc., 1979.

The author offers a step-by-step guidebook to living self-sufficiently. Everything from how to build a greenhouse to how to raise bees.

- Cheek, Donald, *Assertive Black...Puzzled White.* San Luis Obispo, CA: Impact Publishers, Inc., 1976.

Discusses assertiveness from the black perspective. Cheek analyzes the black experience in America and its implications on the concept for "assertiveness" for blacks. Written primarily as a guide for counselors, the book also has many ideas for self help.

- Chesser, Eustace, *Love Without Fear.* NY: New American Library, 1973.

This author discusses the mastery of love-making and the mutual responsibility for marital happiness.

- Comfort, Alex, *Joy of Sex.* NY: Simon & Schuster, Inc., 1980.

A beautifully illustrated source of information, written in non-technical language. It can be read from beginning to end or used as an encyclopedia. The most popular book of its kind.

- Cooper, Cary and Marshall, Judi, *Understanding Executive Stress.* Princeton, NJ: Petrocelli Books, 1978.

The main aim of this book is to provide the reader with a better understanding of the sources of stress acting upon managers in organizations.

- Culligan, Matthew and Sedlacek, Keith, *How to Avoid Stress Before It Kills You.* NY: Gramercy Publishing Co., 1979.

An easy-reading book that presents a well-rounded explanation of stress from the viewpoint of the two authors' lives (a businessman and a physician). The authors provide a wealth of personal experiences to emphasize the concepts.

- de Chardin, Teilhard, *Building the Earth.* Wilkes-Barre, PA: Dimension Books, 1965.

The author was a paleontologist, philosopher, and priest. His vision for the future of the human race is filled with hope, love, and God. This book is written in free verse and creates an optimistic feeling about our potential as individuals and as a world united with a common goal.

- Dinkmeyer, Don and McKay, Gary, *Raising a Responsible Child.* NY: Simon & Schuster, Inc., 1973.

Offers specific family-centered, egalitarian methods that benefit parents as well as children. Helps create a healthy environment for child growth.

- Downing, George, *The Massage Book.* Westminster, MD: Bookworks, 1972.

This book tells you why massage is important and then tells you how to massage each and every part of the body. The drawings are clear and the instructions simple, easy to follow and fun!

- Dreikurs, Rudolf, Gould, Shirley, and Corsini, Raymond, *Family Council.* Chicago: Contemporary Books, Inc., 1974.

The Dreikurs Technique is a way of "putting an end to war" between parents and children (and between children and children). This book is based on the idea that not only are people equal, but that they should be treated as equal. The key is the family council, a problem-solving and communication-building technique. The authors explain, step-by-step and point-by-point, how to introduce the concept into a home.

- Emmons, Michael, *The Inner Source: A Guide to Meditative Therapy.* San Luis Obispo, CA: Impact Publishers, Inc., 1978.

A completely natural approach to holistic health and personal development is presented by this author. He describes, for laypersons and therapists, the steps necessary to experience the "Inner Source," the natural self-healing power within us.

- Ewald, Ellen, *Recipes for a Small Planet.* NY: Ballantine Books, Inc., 1975.

A basic and complete cookbook, in paperback form, it contains hundreds of delicious, body- and planet-conscious recipes for better health, better ecology, and better eating. Companion book: *Diet for a Small Planet.*

- Fanning, Tony and Robbie, *Get It All Done and Still Be Human.* Radnor, PA: Chilton Book Co., 1979.

A quick-reading, handy guide to help you learn to get the most out of your day. There are separate chapters on time-gobblers and how to starve them, time stretchers, and human tools for managing your time.

- Fast, Julius, *The Pleasure Book.* NY: Stein & Day Publishers, 1975.

This is a browsing book. Its goal is to teach the reader how to pursue new pleasures in life by providing one- or two-page explanations of different experiences. The simple pleasures of the wind in your face, day dreaming, white water inner tubing, long baths, perfume and over 60 other potential "peak experiences" come alive on the page, rekindling pleasant memories or creating the desire to try something new. It really is a pleasure book!

- Fensterheim, Herbert and Baer, Jean, *Don't Say Yes When You Want To Say No.* NY: Dell Publishing Co., 1975.

A self-help book that describes a variety of behavioral techniques. Contains practical programs and exercises for overcoming non-assertiveness.

- Fluegelman, A., *The New Games Book.* NY: Doubleday, 1976.

Games for all ages and all sizes of groups. Sometimes a whole community organizes for a New Games Day/Celebration. Emphasis is on pure fun and making everyone feel good. No losers, very few rules. The book has more pictures than instructions; it's fun just to read and enjoy!

- Fonda, Jane, *Jane Fonda's Workout Book.* NY: Simon & Schuster, 1981.

The book has a lot of facts about diet, nutrition and exercise. Photographs demonstrate the routines based on aerobics and stretching.

- Forbes, Rosalind, *Corporate Stress.* Garden City, NY: Doubleday & Co., Inc., 1979.

A very readable, practical book that teaches you how to manage stress on the job and make it work for you. Also deals with organizational stress, stress and job performance, stress and the working woman, and stressful occupations.

- Frankl, Victor, *Man's Search for Meaning.* NY: Washington Square Press, Inc., 1967.

One man's experiences in the concentration camps of Germany. The author explains how he could find life worth living with every possession lost, every value destroyed, suffering from hunger, cold and brutality, expecting extermination hourly.

- Fredericks, Carlton, *Look Younger, Feel Healthier.* NY: Grosset & Dunlap, Inc., 1975.

Learn to make yourself healthier and longer-living through what you eat. That's the purpose of this book, with chapters on nutrition, shelf life, disease prevention, maternity care and infant feeding.

- Freudenberger, Herbert, *Burn Out: How to Beat the High Cost of Success.* NY: Bantam Books, 1981.

This non-technical book provides believable people-stories to illustrate the various forms burn out can take. The most interesting section deals with all those "false cures" some think will help burn out.

- Friedman, Meyer and Rosenman, Ray, *Type A Behavior and Your Heart.* NY: Fawcett Crest Books, 1974.

This book explains what Type A behavior is and how it can lead to coronary heart disease, how to recognize the Type A pattern in your own personality and behavior, and what you can do if you are Type A.

- Gaedwag, Elliott (Ed.), *Inner Balance: The Power of Holistic Healing.* Englewood Cliffs, NJ: Prentice-Hall, Inc., 1979.

This book highlights, through chapters written by thoughtful professionals in the health care system, that a better approach to healing can be achieved through methods of controlling the stress response. The editor's aim was to synthesize three aspects of humans—body, mind, and spirit—specifically related to health and disease.

- Getchell, Bud and Anderson, Wayne, *Being Fit: A Personal Guide.* NY: John Wiley & Sons, Inc., 1982.

Gives the basics on how to become physically fit. Charts rate the benefits of walking, running, swimming, etc.

- Gibran, Kahlil, *The Prophet.* NY: Alfred Knopf, Inc., 1965.

The insight of this author from Lebanon has continued to capture the hearts of humans. Gibran speaks poetically, yet so understandably about everyday life: love, giving, freedom, pain, talking, time, joy, self-knowledge, and other important topics. His words touch the heart and leave a lasting impression.

- Girdano, Daniel and Everly, George, *Controlling Stress and Tension: A Holistic Approach.* Englewood Cliffs, NJ: Prentice-Hall, Inc., 1979.

Part I takes an in-depth look at what stress is, how we come under stress, why we are susceptible to it, and how stress leads to illness. Part II seeks to describe the cause of your stress. What you can do, specifically, to reduce stress in your life is covered in Part III.

SUGGESTED READINGS

- Goldbeck, Nikki and David, *The Supermarket Handbook: Access to Whole Foods.* NY: The New American Library, 1976.

Starting with a shelf-by-shelf tour of what you can find in your local store, this book gives you a complete course in the fine art of label reading; teaches you to recognize the unnecessary additives that raise prices and may be harmful to your health, and provides you with a listing of the best quality foods by brand name. Also includes information about nutrition, whole and natural foods, tried-and-true recipes, saving money on your food budget, and more.

- Goldberg, Phillip and Kaufman, Daniel, *Natural Sleep: How to Get Your Share.* Emmaus, PA: Rodale Press, Inc., 1979.

This is a fun-to-read, meticulously researched book on sleep with effective procedures for achieving sleep without pills. Includes bedtime rituals, massage, breathing and relaxing techniques, hypnosis, herbal remedies, and more.

- Gordon, Thomas, *Parent Effectiveness Training.* NY: David McKay Co., Inc., 1970.

Explains the "no-lose" program for raising responsible children. P.E.T. is a system that incorporates "active listening," "win-win" dialogue, and other techniques to help people live together harmoniously. The system works with children of all ages, including teenagers.

- Greenberg, Herbert, *Coping With Job Stress.* Englewood Cliffs, NJ: Prentice-Hall, Inc., 1980.

This book shows you how to deal effectively with the demands of your job. The author discusses how to break negative habits quickly and permanently. He discusses slowing down, your stress level, why you should indulge yourself, techniques of relieving muscle tension, and much more.

- Greenberg, Robyn, Harmon, Rick and Henshaw, Jean (Eds.), *The Leisure Alternatives Catalog: Food for Mind and Body.* NY: Dell Publishing Co., 1979.

Just browsing through this book is leisure in itself. It contains a large variety of ideas, projects, and adventures to enrich your leisure time. Read it as an idea generator, a dream builder, or as an escape. It contains a wide range of subjects, most with pictures, including mountaineering, cooking, growth experiences, photography, dance, gardening, and on and on.

- Gregg, Elizabeth and Boston Children's Medical Center Staff, *What to Do When There's Nothing to Do.* NY: Dell Publishing Co., 1970.

The Boston Children's Medical Center staff compiled this list of

601 tested play ideas for young children. The creative play ideas are very inexpensive (most do not involve purchases) and are divided into age groups: babies, toddlers, 2-3 year olds, and 3, 4, 5 year olds.

- Grunfeld, Frederick (ed.), *Games of the World: How to Make Them, How to Play Them, How They Came to Be.* NY: Ballantine, 1977.

The title seems to say it all. The colorful, picture-filled book is tantalizing and exciting just to page through. A creative coding system allows you to choose a game to fit your preferences and situation, such as indoor, mind, luck, short preparation time, and other categories.

- Guidelines, *Chronolog: The Time Management Newsletter.* (Box 456, Orinda, CA 94563).

Monthly newsletter details procedures for gaining control of your time. Particularly oriented toward on-the-job situations, special information has appeared on scheduling, meeting procedures, assertiveness, "homework," travel, paperwork management.

- Hall, Francine and Douglas, *The Two-Career Couple.* Reading, MA: Addison-Wesley Publishing Co., 1979.

Combining a relationship and two careers can produce extra stress for a couple. This book offers new research, common sense advice, interviews, and questionnaires to help people cope with the pressure, changes, and conflicts that may result from two careers.

- Hartwig, Daphne, *Make Your Own Groceries.* Indianapolis, IN: Bobbs-Merrill Co., Inc., 1979.

Easy homemade recipes are presented for making foods (and other products) you normally buy at the supermarket, from potato chips to luncheon meat.

- Hastings, Arthur, Fadiman, James and Gordon, James (Eds.), *Health for the Whole Person: The Complete Guide to Holistic Medicine.* NY: Bantam Books, 1980.

If you want a comprehensive source book on holistic approaches to health, this is it. The extensive annotated bibliographies can direct you to the best additional information on such topics as biofeedback, Chinese medicine and acupuncture, natural childbirth, chiropractic, herbal medicines, psychic healing, and nutrition therapy. A very complete review of alternate health techniques.

- Hendricks, Gay and Wills, Russel, *The Centering Book: Awareness Activities for Children, Parents and Teachers.* Englewood Cliffs, NJ: Prentice-Hall, Inc., 1975.

SUGGESTED READINGS

This is an extremely practical and fun collection of awareness activities for children, parents, and teachers. The book teaches meditative exercises, yoga, dream analysis, imagery, physical relaxation, movement activities, relaxing the mind, and more. Appropriate for use with all ages of students from preschool to adult.

- Hutschnecker, Arnold, *The Will to Live.* NY: Simon & Schuster, Inc., 1981.

Originally published in the 50s, this book provides some timely advice on how each person can learn to avoid illness by understanding the emotional disturbances that cause it. The author builds on the basic concept that mind and body are one.

- Jackson, Tom, *Guerrilla Tactics in the Job Market.* NY: Bantam Books, 1978.

Besides clueing you in to the job trends for the 80s, this practical book provides 78 effective tactics to use in landing a satisfying job.

- Jacobson, Howard, *Racewalk to Fitness.* NY: Simon & Schuster, Inc., 1980.

Jacobson has developed a program for "racewalking" which burns calories, develops cardiovascular fitness, tones the upper body and can be done almost anywhere.

- Johnson, June, *838 Ways to Amuse a Child.* NY: Macmillan Publishing Co., Inc., 1962.

This is a valuable collection of crafts, hobbies, and creative ideas for the child from six to twelve. Most suggestions do not depend on elaborate materials, tools, or parental skill.

- Jones, Peter, *How to Cut Heating and Cooling Costs.* NY: Butterick Publishing, 1979.

This book explains how to use the right weatherstripping or caulking for the job, insulate ceilings and walls, install thresholds, choose energy-saving windows or adapt your own, maintain your heating systems for maximum efficiency. Basic, everyday tips every homeowner needs to know.

- Keelan, Jim, *B.S. (Beat Stress) and Live Longer.* Arvada, CO: Communications Unlimited, 1978.

"Too much stress will drive you to the grave or to the nearest mental institution." The goal of this book is to help the reader avoid both of those paths by providing relevant coping tools which can create a sound mind in a healthy body. The book is straightforward, humorous, candid, and conversational in directing the reader through the process of recognizing personal stressors and doing something about them.

- Kinzer, Nora, *Stress and the American Woman.* NY: Doubleday Books, Inc., 1979.

The author illuminates the factors, symptoms and situations of stress which a woman faces both in the business world and at home. Begins with a detailed description of the origins of stress and the response of a woman's body. The author explores the tensions of adopting "male behavior" to achieve success, a woman's "natural" guards against stress, the dilemma of femininity, and the special problems of female physiology and motherhood.

- Kostrubala, Thaddeus, *Joy of Running.* NY: J.B. Lippincott Co., 1976.

A paperback that emphasizes the spiritual, physical and psychological aspects of running.

- Krantzler, Mel, *Creative Divorce.* NY: M. Evans & Co., 1974.

This book deals with the feelings of men and women facing the need to build new lives in the crisis of divorce.

- Kubler-Ross, Elisabeth, *Death: The Final Stage of Growth.* Englewood Cliffs, NJ: Prentice-Hall, Inc., 1975.

From her own personal views and experiences and from comparisons with how various cultures view death and dying, Kubler-Ross answers such questions as: Why do we treat death as a taboo? What are the sources of our fears? How do we express our grief and accept the death of a person close to us? How can we prepare for our own death? She shows how, through an acceptance of our finiteness, we can grow, for death provides a key to the meaning of human existence.

- Kubler-Ross, Elisabeth, *On Death and Dying.* NY: Macmillan Publishing Co., Inc., 1964.

Dr. Ross attempts to focus on the dying patient so that we can all learn from that patient the anxieties, fears and hopes of dying.

- Kuntzleman, Charles T., *Diet Free.* Emmaus, PA: Rodale Press, 1982.

Based on the theory that the best way to lose weight is to engage in a program of increased activity.

- Kuzma, Kay, *Prime-Time Parenting.* NY: Rawson, Wade Publishers, Inc., 1980.

An innovative, comprehensive program for busy parents. It offers a unique perspective on parenting, plus hundreds of practical suggestions and exercises. Chapter 9, "Shortcuts to Prime-Time Parenting," is especially creative and helpful.

- Lakein, Alan, *How to Get Control of Your Time and Your Life.* NY: New American Library, 1974.

An excellent guide to managing personal and business time. The author explains how to set short and long-term goals, establish priorities, organize a daily schedule and achieve better self-understanding. Tips are included on building willpower, creating quiet time, defeating unpleasant tasks, and keeping yourself on target.

- Lange, Arthur and Jakubowski, Patricia, *Responsible Assertive Behavior.* Champaign, IL: Research Press, 1976.

This book is really two separate texts. First, a manual for assertion trainers and second, a self-help book for those who want to become more assertive. It includes a variety of exercises and examples and systematic strategies for changing behavior.

- Lappe, Frances Moore, *Diet for a Small Planet.* NY: Ballantine Books, Inc., 1975.

A very detailed paperback that tells you what foods to put together to make delicious protein-rich meals without heavy use of meats; why you must have protein, and how much; cost comparisons of non-meat protein; recipes, charts that demonstrate a whole new world of protein eating. Companion book: *Recipes for a Small Planet.* Both are dedicated to the concept of meat complementarity—obtaining high quality, complete protein by the right combinations of legumes, grains, seeds and dairy products.

- LeShan, Lawrence, *How to Meditate: A Guide to Self-Discovery.* Boston: Little, Brown & Co., 1974.

This book has a simple, straightforward approach that demystifies meditation. The content covers psychological effects, basic types, structured and unstructured, as well as choosing your own meditation path.

- LeShan, Lawrence, *You Can Fight for Your Life: Emotional Factors in the Treatment of Cancer.* NY: M. Evans & Co., 1980.

The author offers new evidence and insights into why some individuals get cancer while others do not—and why some are able to fight successfully for their lives while others give up. The connection between the emotions and cancer should be of interest to the patient and his/her family as well as to doctors, nurses, counselors, and clergy.

- Mackenzie, R. Alec, *The Time Trap.* NY: McGraw-Hill Book Co., Inc., 1975.

This book has practical, easy-to-apply tips and techniques for overcoming the problems of procrastination, interruptions, decision-making, organization and delegation. Helpful to people in business, managers of all kinds of organizations, secretaries, teachers, public officials—all who want to make the most of time.

- Mandino, Og, *The Greatest Miracle in the World.* NY: Bantam Books, 1975.

The books of Og Mandino are short but powerful. In this book we meet Simon Potter, a mystic ragpicker. He shares an amazing "Memorandum" from God. The memo is to every reader who is interested in personal happiness and success. The message is simple but potentially life-changing.

- Martin, Elizabeth, *The Over-30; 6-Week All Natural Health and Beauty Plan.* NY: Clarkson N. Potter, Inc., 1982.

The plan tackles health and beauty with a 30-minute-a-day regime that includes yoga, calisthenics, stretching and weight lifting.

- Martinez, Pam, *Sugarless Cooking.* Issaquah, WA: Medic Publishing Co., 1977.

A good variety of recipes are printed in easy-to-read type. The book shows how to cook everything from appetizers to vegetables without sugar.

- Maskowitz, Robert, *How to Organize Your Work and Your Life.* Garden City, NY: Doubleday & Co., 1981.

The author takes up where Alan Lakein leaves off with his book, *How to Get Control of Your Time and Your Life.* Filled with individual time management programs, worksheets, and a unique index of time management problems and remedies so you can cure your own particular problems. A good resource for coping with special problems as they arise.

- McQuade, Walter and Aikman, Ann, *Stress.* NY: Bantam Books, 1975.

This book examines the causes of stress in career crises, family pressures, and urban living. It offers solutions to the problems of stress, including a four-point anti-stress program that anyone, no matter how busy, can follow.

- Millman, Dan, *Whole Body Fitness: Training Mind, Body, and Spirit.* NY: Clarkson N. Potter, Inc., 1979.

This book is for *everyone* interested in the benefits of physical activity. The author combines the wisdom and training practices of the East and West into a natural training process for developing the mind, body and spirit.

- Moody, Raymond, *Life After Life.* Covington, GA: Mockingbird Books, Inc., 1975.

Those who have been clinically dead and then revived seem to share common experiences. The accounts of more than 100 subjects were compiled. The testimony is startlingly similar in detail and seems to provide some insights into the existence of the human spirit beyond death.

- Nyad, Diana and Hogan, Candice Lyle, *Diana Nyad's Basic Training for Women.* NY: Crown Publishers, Inc., 1981.

This book presents a program based on aerobic activity, stretching and weight training that takes 30 minutes a day. Helps develop physical changes: less fat, firmer thighs and better skin tone.

- Orbach, Susie, *Fat is a Feminist Issue.* NY: Berkley, 1979.

A self-help guide for compulsive eaters, this book is about protection, sex, mothering, strength, assertion, and love. Explains why fat is a response to the way women are seen by their husbands, their mothers, their bosses, and themselves. Teaches the difference between "Mouth hunger" and "stomach hunger."

- Peale, Norman Vincent, *The Power of Positive Thinking.* NY: Prentice-Hall, Inc., 1956.

This is a classic that remains popular for only one reason—the ideas work! Dr. Peale demonstrates the power of faith in action. A proper attitude can change lives and win success in all things. This book outlines the steps to achieve any goal.

- Pelletier, Kenneth, *Mind as Healer, Mind as Slayer.* NY: Dell Publishing Co., Inc., 1977.

A holistic approach to preventing stress disorders. The book's three major sections include a survey of the sources of stress, guidelines for the evaluation of one's own stress levels, profiles of various disease-prone personalities, and a practical section concerned with the prevention of stress-related diseases through such techniques as meditation and biofeedback.

- Phelan, Nancy and Volin, Michael, *Yoga for Women.* NY: Perennial Lib., 1973.

A photographically-illustrated book for women of all ages who wish to use yoga for improvement of physical and mental states.

- Phelps, Stanlee and Austin, Nancy, *The Assertive Woman.* San Luis Obispo, CA: Impact Publishers, Inc., 1975.

A clearly written book for a systematic attack upon the self-denying lifestyle so many women have been conditioned to accept.

- Porter, Sylvia, *Sylvia Porter's New Money Book for the 80's.* Garden City, New York: Doubleday, 1979.

A simple guide to consumer economics, beginning with basics.

- Powell, John, *The Secret of Staying in Love.* Niles, IL: Argus, 1974.

The "secret" is communication. Your greatest gift to another is a gift of yourself through the honest sharing of feelings and emotions. The prerequisite to this personal sharing is a joyful acceptance of self.

- Powell, John, *Why Am I Afraid to Love?* Niles, IL: Argus Communications, 1972.

The capacity to love is within all of us. John Powell's perceptive and candid style makes it possible to release that power.

- Quinn, Jane Bryant, *Everyone's Money Book.* NY: Dell Publishing Co., 1980.

A comprehensive book that clearly explains just about everything you can do with your money including saving, borrowing, investing, earning. Over 800 pages of advice on home buying and selling, creative checking accounts, income taxes and more.

- Rodale Press, Emmaus, PA, *Executive Fitness Newsletter.*

A biweekly, covers such topics as: how to keep from gaining weight on the road, exercise and arthritis.

- Rogers, Carl, *Becoming Partners: Marriage and Its Alternatives.* NY: Dell Publishing Co., 1973.

Using interviews in the partners' own words, Rogers gives a series of slices, pictures, perceptions—of relationships, breakdowns, restructuring—in a wide variety of partnerships. These are followed by his own commentary and summation. Nonjudgmental reviews of the author's own marriage, conventional, long-lived, and successful; commune group marriages; a triangle; a quartet; and a racially mixed marriage.

- Ruff, Howard, *How to Prosper During the Coming Bad Years.* NY: Times Books, 1979.

This is a valuable crash course in personal and financial survival. Contains specific investment techniques to combat the erosion of your savings; prescribes solid, easily-understood, easily-managed investment plans as hedges against inflation.

- Ryan, Regina and Travis, John, *Wellness Workbook.* Berkeley, CA: Ten Speed Press, 1981.

Once you have completed *StressMap*, the *Wellness Workbook* is highly recommended as a follow up. It will teach you how to transcend and go beyond the basics in breathing, communicating, eating, *playing*, finding meaning, moving, thinking, sensing, and feeling. It is really a fun workbook filled with priceless tidbits of insight and information.

- Samuels, Mike and Bennett, Hal, *Be Well.* NY: Random House, Inc., 1975.

In a fast and easy-to-read book, the authors describe the manner in which the body heals itself and what a person can do to increase healing by an attitude that centers on well-being. Feelings are isolated as guides to health or its absence, and approaches for getting in touch with feelings that result in ease are outlined.

- Schlayer, Mary and Cooley, Marilyn, *How to Be a Financially Secure Woman.* NY: Ballantine Books, Inc., 1978.

Solid financial advice aimed specifically at women—young, old, single, married, executive, homemaker—by a female financial expert. Information on everything from setting up a household budget to high-powered investing.

- Selye, Hans, *Stress Without Distress.* NY: New American Library, 1975.

Dr. Selye synthesizes a lot of information on stress control and provides a framework for examination and refinement of your own sense of purpose. He reinforces ideas of self-responsibility and individual uniqueness in dealing with stress.

- Sheehy, Gail, *Passages: Predictable Crises of Adult Life.* NY: Bantam Books, 1977.

This book shows you how men and women continue growing up as adults from 18 to 50. There are predictable crises at each step. The steps are the same for both sexes, but the developmental rhythms are not. Understanding this, we can use each crisis to stretch ourselves to our full potential instead of holding ourselves or our partners to blame.

- Simonton, O. Carl, Matthews-Simonton, Stephanie and Creighton, James, *Getting Well Again.* NY: Bantam Books, 1980.

The authors profile the typical "cancer personality" and how positive expectations, self-awareness and self-care can contribute to survival. This very readable, exciting book offers the same self-help techniques the Simontons' patients have used so successfully to reinforce usual medical treatment—techniques for learning positive attitudes, relaxation, visualization, goal setting, managing pain, exercise, and building an emotional support system. The best aspect of this book is that it is not only for cancer patients or others with serious illness but for *anyone* who wants to participate in maintaining his or her health.

- Stein, Lincoln, *Family Games.* NY: Macmillan Publishing Co., Inc., 1979.

With pictures and drawings, this book explains the basics of playing games anywhere as a family or with a group. Stein covers card games, tricks, picnic games, street games, party games and more. He seems to include everything from frisbee to musical chairs to computer games.

- Terkel, Studs, *Working*. NY: Avon Books, 1975.

Through hundreds of interviews, the author acquired insights and straight facts about a good cross-section of the American work force. An excellent resource for anyone interested in some inside info about a career field.

- U.S. Government Printing Office, Washington, DC, *A Guide to Budgeting for the Family*.

A short, inexpensive bulletin that can help you develop and implement a budget that is tailored to immediate needs and long-range goals. Practical advice and step-by-step methods for estimating income and expenses, setting up a budget, keeping records and more. Includes a handy chart for recording expenses. (U.S. Government Publication S/N 001-000-03514-2 available from Supt. of Documents, U.S.G.P.O., Washington, DC 20402.)

- U.S. Government Printing Office, Washington, DC, *An Introduction to Running: One Step at a Time*.

This booklet provides basic information needed before beginning a running program. Includes advice on running style, warming up and cooling down, where to run, wearing apparel, and much more. (U.S. Government Publication S/N 017-001-00425-1.)

- U.S. Government Printing Office, Washington, DC, *How to Buy Food*.

An inexpensive kit containing 14 illustrated booklets to help you get the most for your money. Practical advice on what to look for when you shop, how to judge quality, whether to buy bulk quantities, much more. (U.S. Govt. Publication S/N 001-016-00090-3).

- Vaughn, William, *Low Salt Secrets for Your Diet*. NY: Warner Books, 1981.

Only 3½ x 5 inches, this handy, carry-along guide tells you where the salt is hidden in the foods you buy. Contains an up-to-date, easy-to-use listing of the sodium content in over 2,000 brand-name and natural foods.

- Volin, Michael and Phelan, Nancy, *Yoga for Beauty*. NY: Arc Books, 1971.

A practical book in which the authors deal with methods and techniques to improve the beauty of the face and body, as well as inner beauty.

- Walker, C. Eugene, *Learn to Relax: 13 Ways to Reduce Tension*. Englewood Cliffs, NJ: Prentice-Hall, Inc., 1975.

Demonstrates 13 ways to reduce tension. The author also explains helpful problem-solving and decision-making systems that can keep you from feeling overwhelmed.

SUGGESTED READINGS

- Weinstein, Matt and Goodman, Joel, *Playfair: Everybody's Guide to Non-Competitive Play.* San Luis Obispo, CA: Impact Publishers, Inc., 1980.

    Playfair is a delightful excuse to have more fun. Detailed plans for 60 simple and complex games for everyone. The emphasis here is on FUN, not winning. The book is fun to read, fun to use, and more fun to share.

- Welch, I. David, Medeiros, Donald, and Tate, George, *Beyond Burnout.* Englewood Cliffs, NJ: Prentice-Hall, Inc., 1982.

    What happens when dedicated and committed people begin to actively dislike their work, their coworkers, and their bosses? This book explains why people in 13 different occupations burn out, lists the symptoms to look for, and provides an extensive section of suggestions for cures in specific occupations.

- Wolfe, Ralph and Clegg, Peter, *Home Energy for the Eighties.* Charlotte, VT: Garden Way Publishing Co., 1979.

    Two "energy architects" explain solar energy, water power, wind power and wood heating—and especially home energy conservation. Comparisons of current products. Lists 400 resources.

- Yates, Jere, *Managing Stress.* NY: American Management Assn., Inc., 1980.

    The author specifically addresses the manager's concern with effectively managing his/her own stress as well as that of the people under his/her supervision.

Serving Human Development Since 1970

We hope you have enjoyed reading this book. For more books with "IMPACT," we invite you to consider the following titles...

YOUR PERFECT RIGHT
A Guide to Assertive Living [6th Edition]
by Robert E. Alberti, Ph.D. and
Michael L. Emmons, Ph.D.

THE assertiveness classic, now updated and completely rewritten. Chapters on assertive sexuality, assertiveness at work, goal-setting, anger, relationships, anxiety management, dealing with difficult people. Totally revised, this SIXTH EDITION has more than double the material of the original 1970 edition.
Softcover $8.95/Hardcover $12.95 Book No. 10-0

THE ASSERTIVE WOMAN
A New Look
by Stanlee Phelps, M.S.W. and
Nancy Austin, M.B.A.

Completely revised and updated second edition of the classic. Over a quarter-million copies of the original provided inspiration and encouragement to women and groups. New expanded discussions of careers, individuality, children, relationships (lovers, family, friends), and more.
Softcover $8.95 Book No. 61-5

REBUILDING
When Your Relationship Ends
by Bruce Fisher, Ed.D.

A book for those who are putting their lives back together after divorce or after other crises. **Rebuilding** includes aids for coping with the fifteen "building blocks" that mark the path to recovery: denial, loneliness, guilt, rejection, grief, anger, letting go, self-concept, friendships, leftover love, trust, sexuality, responsibility, singleness and freedom.
Softcover $8.95 Book No. 30-5

THE COUPLE'S JOURNEY
Intimacy as a Path to Wholeness
by Susan M. Campbell, Ph.D.

"Coupling, like life, is a continually changing process." Dr. Campbell guides us on the five-stage path of growth traveled by every intimate relationship: romance, power struggle, stability, commitment and co-creation. Here is help in discovering new meaning in the often confusing process of living intimately with another person.
Softcover $7.95 Book No. 45-3

PLAYFAIR
Everybody's Guide to Non-Competitive Play
by Matt Weinstein, Ph.D. and
Joel Goodman, Ed.D.

Now you can play games where EVERYONE wins! Sixty non-competitive games for large and small groups, adults, young adults, schools, children, families. Detailed descriptions with complete instructions for "play-leaders." A delightful book that takes play seriously and makes it a way of life; filled with playful photographs!
Softcover $10.95 Book No. 50-X

SURVIVING WITH KIDS
A Lifeline for Overwhelmed Parents
by Wayne Bartz, Ph.D. and
Richard Rasor, Ed.D.

A jargon-free, practical book for parents! Thirty proven principles of behavior applied to parent-child interaction. Clearly written, down-to-earth, and delightfully illustrated with cartoon-style examples of everyday situations. A solid guide for first-time parents and those who sometimes feel overwhelmed... and isn't that everybody?
Softcover $8.95 Book No. 55-0

DON'T SWEAT THE SMALL STUFF
P.S. It's All Small Stuff
by Michael R. Mantell, Ph.D.

Collection of short articles from a well-known media psychologist on dozens of life problems: alcohol, anxiety, divorce, drugs, illness, parenting, relationships...more. Written in popular, friendly style, yet based on the latest psychological research.
Softcover $8.95 Book No. 56-9

NO MORE SECRETS
Protecting Your Child from Sexual Assault
by Caren Adams and Jennifer Fay

A supportive, conversational guide for parents who wish to teach their young children how to prevent sexual advances. Points out that most offenders are not strangers but relatives and "friends." This important resource encourages open discussion — "no secrets" — between parents and children. Dialogue, games and other tools to help parents instruct children 3 and up.
Softcover $4.95 Book No. 24-0

LIKING MYSELF
by Pat Palmer, Ed.D.
Illustrated by Betty Shondeck

A child-size introduction to concepts of feelings, self-esteem and assertiveness for youngsters 5-9. Delightful drawings help convey its message to young readers. **Liking Myself** is widely used by parents and teachers to help children learn and appreciate the good things about themselves, their feelings and their behavior.
Softcover $4.95; w/Teacher Guide $6.95
Book No. 41-0

THE MOUSE, THE MONSTER & ME!
Assertiveness for Young People
by Pat Palmer, Ed.D.
Illustrated by Betty Shondeck

Assertiveness concepts for youngsters 8 and up explained in an entertaining way. Non-assertive "mice" and aggressive "monsters" offer young persons an opportunity to develop a sense of personal rights and responsibilities, to become appropriately assertive and to gain a greater sense of self-worth.
Softcover $4.95; w/Teacher Guide $6.95
Book No. 43-7

STRESSMAP: Finding Your Pressure Points
by Michele Haney, Ph.D. and
Edmond Boenisch, Ph.D.

A personal guidebook for pinpointing sources of stress — and finding stress relief! Questionnaire "maps" help readers survey people, money, work, body, mind and leisure stress areas. New second edition devotes chapter to recognizing, preventing and treating burnout. Worksheets permit an individualized plan for relief.
Softcover $7.95 Book No. 60-7

LEAD ON! The Complete Handbook For Group Leaders
by Leslie G. Lawson, Ph.D.,
Franklyn Donant, M.A., and John Lawson, Ed.D.

Comprehensive guide for leaders of volunteer groups. Twenty-four easy to follow chapters make it easy to lead. Describes essentials for novices and experienced leaders. Indispensable for leaders of youth clubs, church programs, and other "new volunteerism" organizations.
Softcover $7.95 Book No. 27-5

THE STOP SMOKING BOOK
by Margaret Kraker McKean

Lends a gentle helping hand to smokers who have chosen to quit. Humor and humanness — no lectures or shock treatment. Twenty-five personalized Ways lend warm support to "the choice to be stronger than cigarettes."
Softcover $6.95 Book No. 59-3

Please see the following page for more books and information on how to order.

Impact Publishers

... more books with "IMPACT"

BEYOND THE POWER STRUGGLE
Dealing With Conflict in Love and Work
by Susan M. Campbell, Ph.D.

Explores relationship issues from the viewpoint that, "Differences are inevitable, but conflict and struggle are not." Helps expand perspectives on relationships in love and at work. Psychologist Campbell challenges us to see both sides of a conflict by seeing both sides of ourselves. A creative and thoughtful analysis, accompanied by specific exercises to help relationships grow.
Softcover $8.95   Book No. 46-1

NO IS NOT ENOUGH
Helping Teenagers Avoid Sexual Assault
by Caren Adams, Jennifer Fay and
Jan Loreen-Martin

Guidebook for parents provides proven, realistic strategies to help teens avoid victimization: acquaintance rape, exploitation by adults, touching, influence of media, peer pressures. Includes a primer on **what** to say and **when**. Tells how to provide teens with information they need to recognize compromising situations and skills they need to resist pressure.
Softcover $7.95   Book No. 35-6

WORKING FOR PEACE: A Handbook of Practical Psychology And Other Tools
Neil Wollman, Ph.D., Editor

Thirty-five chapter collection of guidelines, ideas and suggestions for improving effectiveness of peace work activities for individuals and groups. Written by psychologists and other experts in communication, speech, and political science.
Softcover $9.95   Book No. 37-2

MARITAL MYTHS: Two Dozen Mistaken Beliefs That Can Ruin A Marriage [Or Make A Bad One Worse]
by Arnold A. Lazarus, Ph.D.

Twenty-four myths of marriage are exploded by a world-reknowned psychologist/marital therapist who has treated hundreds of relationships in over 25 years of practice. Full of practical examples and guidance for self-help readers who want to improve their own marriages.
Softcover $6.95   Book No. 51-8

WHEN MEN ARE PREGNANT
Needs and Concerns of Expectant Fathers
by Jerrold Lee Shapiro, Ph.D.

The first in-depth guide for men who are "expecting." Based on interviews with over 200 new fathers. Covers the baby decision, stages of pregnancy, physical and emotional factors, childbirth, and the first six weeks of fatherhood.
Softcover $8.95   Book No. 62-3

KNOWING WHEN TO QUIT
by Jack Barranger, M.A.

Guide to getting out of counter-productive situations in work, relationships. Quitting can be a courageous act. Helps reader evaluate what's really going on in a situation, formulate options, and make a well-considered decision to stay or quit.
Softcover $8.95   Book No. 57-7

TEEN ESTEEM: A Self-Direction Manual for Young Adults
by Pat Palmer, Ed.D. with
Melissa Alberti Froehner

Emphasizes self-esteem and self-direction for teens who need refusal skills and positive attitudes to handle peer pressure, substance abuse, sexual expression, other teen problems. Easy to read, evaluated by teens and shaped by their feedback. Cartoon illustrations.
Softcover $6.95   Book No. 66-6

WHAT DO I DO WHEN...? A Handbook for Parents and Other Beleaguered Adults
by Juliet V. Allen, M.A.

"A parent's hotline in handbook." Ready-reference answers to over 50 childrearing dilemmas. Comprehensive, practical, common-sense solutions that **really work**. Short on theory, long on practical solutions to crying, fighting, bedwetting, car behavior, self-esteem, shyness, working parents, discipline, and much, much more.
Softcover $8.95   Book No. 23-2

TRUST YOURSELF— You Have The Power: A Holistic Handbook for Self-Reliance
by Tony Larsen, D. Min.

Dr. Larsen, teacher, counselor and Unitarian-Universalist minister, demonstrates how each of us has the power to handle our world. This can be done in a completely natural way and depends only upon the power which we already possess.
Softcover $8.95   Book No. 18-6

LIFE CHANGES
Growing Through Personal Transitions
by Sabina A. Spencer, M.S. and
John D. Adams, Ph.D.

Recession, military actions, layoffs, mergers and acquisitions, plant closings — social and economic changes are unpredictable and in-evitable. And personal transitions abound: births, deaths, divorce, retirement, relocation. **Life Changes** is the essential survival manual for understanding and coping with change.
Softcover $8.95   Book No. 68-2

YOU CAN BEAT DEPRESSION
A Guide To Recovery
by John Preston, Psy.D.

Concise, readable... offers easy access to help for people in need. Clinical psychologist guides readers in self-assessment and how to use appropriate self-help or find professional treatment. An authoritative guide for every depressed person, and anybody who cares about one.
Softcover $8.95   Book No.64-X

GETTING APART TOGETHER: The Couple's Guide to a Fair Divorce or Separation
by Martin Kranitz, M.A.

Couples can save time, money, heartache by preparing their own fair settlement **before they see an attorney**. Procedures for cooperative negotiation of co-parenting, custody, property, support, insurance, finances, taxes. Includes agendas, forms.
Softcover $8.95   Book. No. 58-5

SEND FOR OUR FREE CATALOG

Impact Publishers' books are available at booksellers throughout the U.S.A. and in many other countries. If you are not able to find a title of interest at a nearby bookstore, we would be happy to fill your direct order. Please send us:
1. Complete name, address and zip code information
2. The full title and book no.'s of the book(s) you want
3. The number of copies of each book
4. California residents add 6-1/4% sales tax
5. Add $2.25 shipping for the first book; $.25 for each additional book VISA or MasterCard are acceptable; be sure to include complete card number, expiration date, and your authorizing signature.
Prices effective January 1991, and subject to change without notice.
Send your order to: **Impact Publishers**™
P.O. Box 1094, San Luis Obispo, CA 93406
[805] 543-5911